Beasts of the Forest, Beasts of the Field

Matt Pavelich

Seattle

Owl Creek Press

ACKNOWLEDGMENTS

A part of "After the Ten Bend Rodeo" was published in *Special Report: Fiction* magazine, copyright 1990.

"Tacoma" appeared in slightly different form in *Sequoia.*

Cover art: "Running III" by Diana Ostby

Owl Creek Press
1620 N. 45th St.
Seattle WA 98103

CONTENTS

This volume is published by the Montana Arts Council as the winning selection in the 1989 First Book Award Competition. Funding for this project was received, in part, from the National Endowment for the Arts.

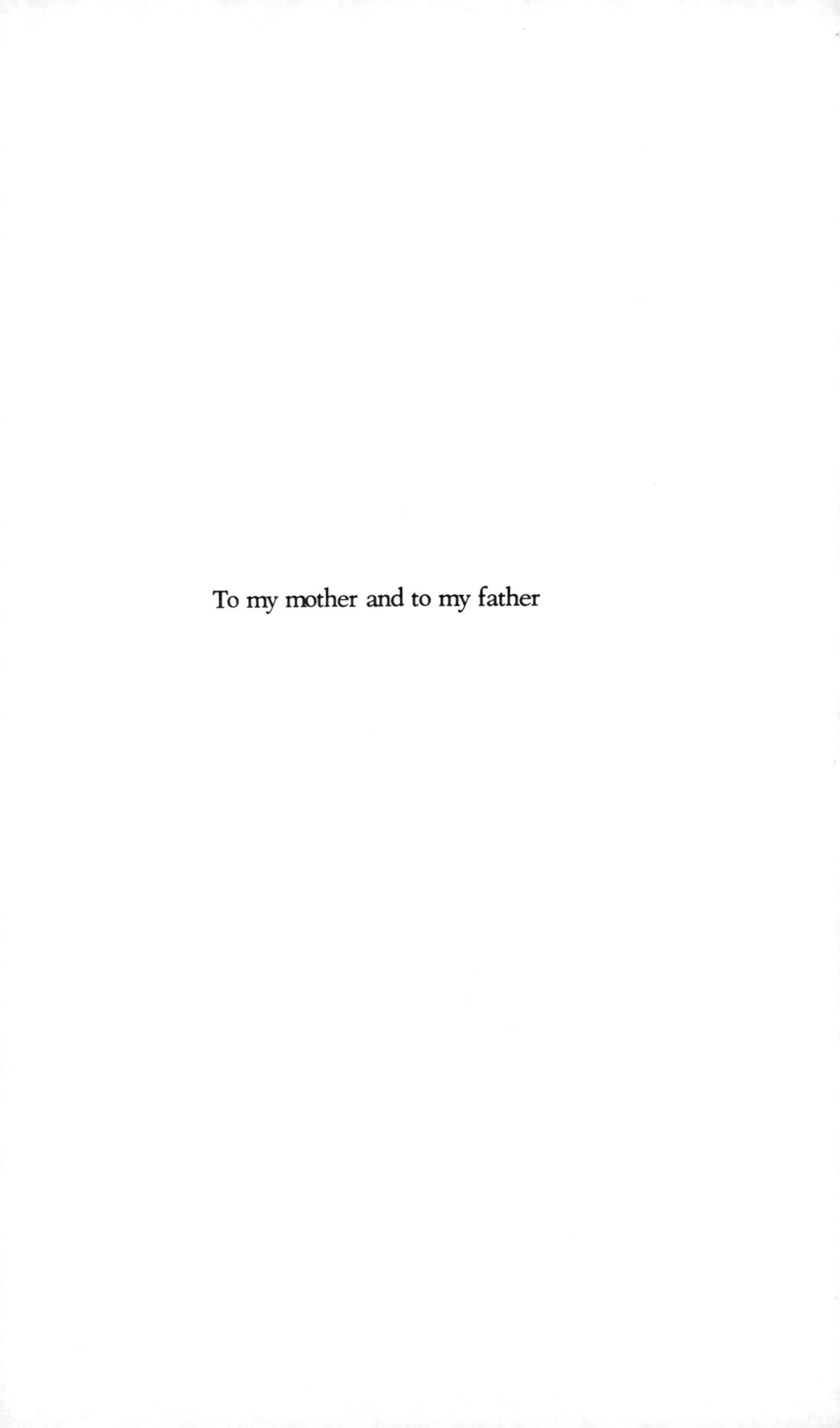

To my mother and to my father

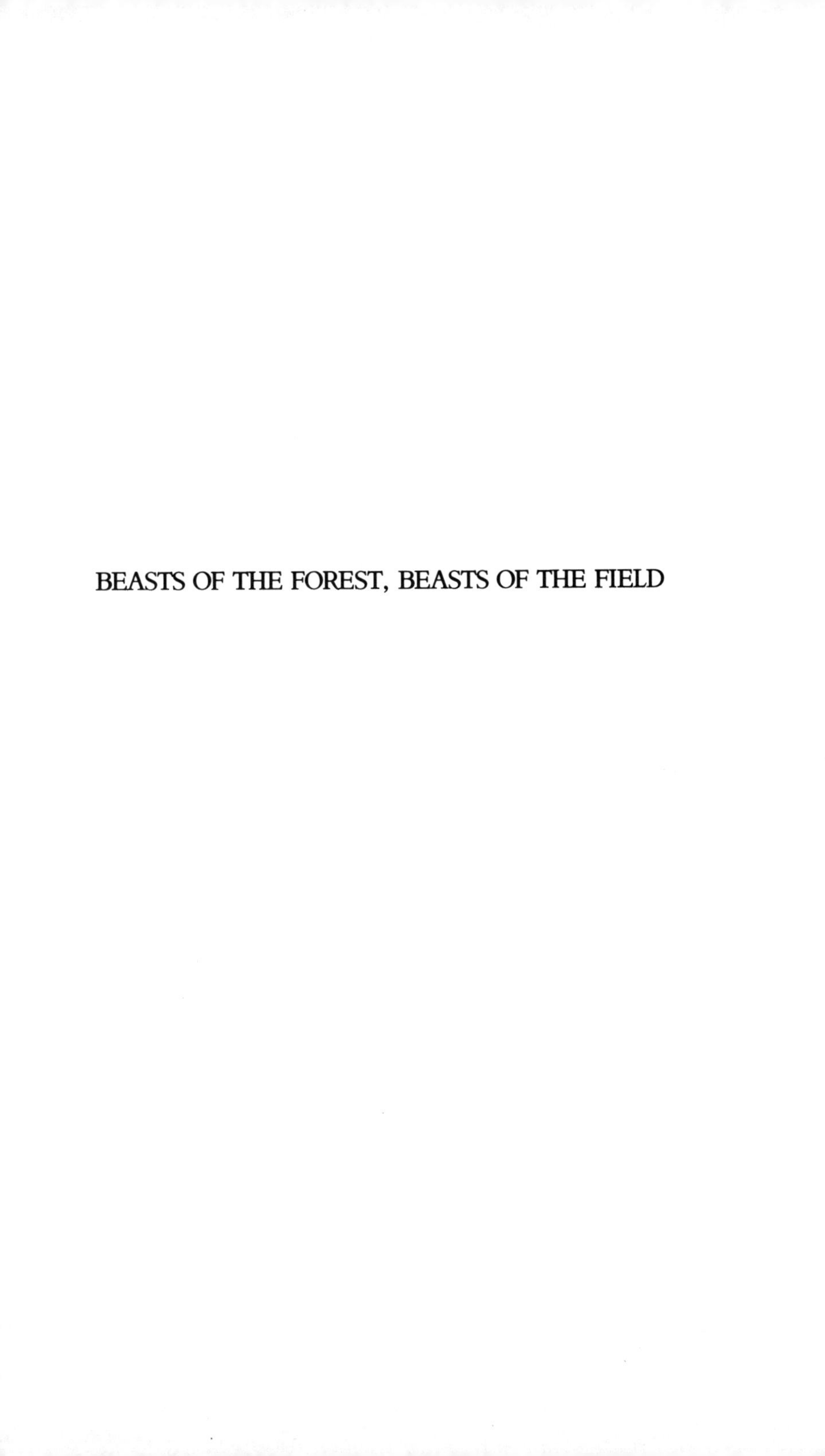

BEASTS OF THE FOREST, BEASTS OF THE FIELD

AFTER THE TEN BEND RODEO

1.

We jumped at the same time, with the same motion. The summer we were sixteen, Ernie Evans and I jumped from the superstructure of the Charlo Street bridge into the Laughing Man River. Our left knees lifted like dancers' in a chorus line, our right feet shoved hard away from the girder, the river whelmed. All sinew, we made a neat hole, falling--feet first and fast at the light-spackled water, arms out circling for balance. We felt our souls turn bouyant or reluctant, and we fell away from them too. Beautifully empty, we hit the river.

It was a generous season, as I recall, elsewhere. Not many fires in the woods, and people from other valleys were hauling hay they wouldn't need to the Dakotas. In the hardscrabble corner of the reservation, though, the promising clouds all passed over to spill when they caught on the Mission range. Around Ten Bend there was one spare cutting of alfalfa, a lot of Russian thistle, and two halfbreed babies were born that summer. Most expected better from the hardpan, no matter how many times they'd been disappointed. Toward the end of August, when the sky was so blue that it tended toward purple well before dusk and well after dawn--a heartbreak blue--the rodeo and pow-wow were held.

I can't remember a better weekend. A dogfight every hour. On Friday, two flatbed trucks came down the street, one loaded with the Live Wire 4H Club, another with Original Homesteaders. Then Billy Johnson astride a popping two-cycle scooter that made him unpopular with the riders behind him. Skittish horses. Horseshoes ringing off the pavement, being pitched against stakes. Games. Harvey Breslaw ran flights of kids up and down the street with his bullhorn, two-legged, three-legged, and backward--a silver dollar to every winner. Rodeo cowboys with tape on their boots, working cowboys with their hands two knuckles deep in the pockets of their jeans. Music came from every direction, and at no time of the night would it completely fade away--Ray Halberding, still working his squeeze box when the birds began to sing. And so much food. So many women who'd been waiting for this chance to be pretty where it might matter. Drunk or sober, it was easy to decide during rodeo weekend that certain mistakes had waited too long to be made.

Because my dad owned the Oasis and my bedroom was above the only decent dance floor in Ten Bend, my sleep in those days was filled with the bass parts of the country tunes that pulsed up through the ceiling, and I learned early how lamentable and thin was the wisdom of my elders. I was there the night a catskinner from Kalispell chewed off Jimmy Van Horne's ear, the night Mrs. McCready spit pickled pigs' feet on her husband. I was made to haul beer like a Chinaman. But there were times, that rodeo weekend was one of them, when my chores at the Oasis were the keys to the kingdom. Saturday night, a woman I'd never seen before stopped me as I was wheeling a keg through the crowd, and she gave me a ten dollar bill--reparation, I suppose, for some distant failure. I also found a twenty on the floor of the men's room. It was perfectly dry.

So I walked out the next morning, muzzy-headed for lack of sleep, to the north edge of town, across the bridge, and into the shimmering dome of alkali dust above the rodeo arena and the pow-wow grounds. The drums were going at the pow-wow, monotonous and irresistible. I bought a soda and some jerked meat at a booth, and I went for them.

Two squaws, melted-looking women in print dresses, pounded at big flat drums. They were driving a pair of young dancers around in a circle under the shade of a tarpaulin, a long-legged kid, rigged out in beaded buckskin, and a rounder one with his belly bouncing off the waistband of a pair of bellbottoms. The chunky kid was the better dancer. He saw me standing there and gave me a hard look. Blackfoot, I thought; I lived among Kootenai, and they held that the Blackfeet were a sullen people. I was trying out a hard look of my own when I felt someone's foot nudging the back of my knee. Luther Pablo, my unnecessary friend. Luther with the slick line of fur on his upper lip. "What're you doin'?" he asked me.

"Nothin'," I said, glad for an excuse to turn away from the dancer.

"You wanna do somethin'?"

"What?"

"Got any money?"

"No," I said. But I think he had already smelled it on me. He claimed to know of big opportunities. Soon we were among the crowd at the edge of the stick game. "That's Agnes Hewankorn," he told me. "You know who she is?"

"Your relation," I said. He was related to almost everyone.

"Yeah, on Mom's side. She makes her livin' at this, so you know she don't lose much." Stick game players knelt along the length of two lodge poles laid parallel on the ground, about four feet apart. Agnes, a woman who seemed old to me but was probably not more than forty, sat in a salad of bills she clearly cared nothing for. "She'll play for you," Luther said. "You could be on her side."

"If you . . . it's like a side bet?"

"You got some money, ain't it? You been lyin'."

Another game started then. The players along both lodge poles started chanting, beating out a cadence with little sticks. I asked Luther, "How do I get in?" He held out his hand. I put my ten in it and his hand just hovered there. I added my twenty. He gave both to Agnes, and she crumpled them, threw them onto a pile assembling between the lodge poles. There was no obvious system of accounting in this, money just heaped up. The chanting got louder and, it seemed to me, more purposeful. To most of us, the game was a rhythmic mystery. Agnes extended her arm like a sorceress and followed the progress of a pair of bearbone dice being passed up and down the rank of players across from her. The dice came to a man with a crew cut and a heavily seamed face, or they appeared to. Coyly the man kneaded the contents of his hands--he'd show them, hide them. Agnes watched him. He watched her. Now the chanting came louder, faster. Agnes looked to be working a hex on the man. She pointed at his left hand.

"Heey yah," he yelled, and he threw the dice in his right hand out onto the money pile. It was the blue one.

Agnes' head rocked back. A high, strangled expression of disbelief came from her.

"Luther?"

Agnes recovered at once, and was laughing.

"Luther?"

The crew cut man raked my money, along with the rest of the pot, toward him.

"Wow," said Luther quizzically. "You wanna go over to the rodeo, Pete? I know a way we can get in for free."

"Fuck you, man."

"Gee," he said, "you white guys should never gamble."

I was out my windfall. The money had never seemed real, anyway. But now I was susceptible to more of Luther's strange entertainments. His next plan had us crossing the quarter mile between the pow-wow grounds and the rodeo arena, moving low through washes, behind sagebrush, sometimes on our knees. He favored drama over necessity. To support this particular fun we had to pretend that a jackpot rodeo was being jealously guarded. The last leg of our route took us under the bed of a stock truck. We were in. In, as it turned out, right behind a cowgirl wearing cowgirl pants. They fit her faithfully as her skin, might have been her skin if they weren't lavender.

"Whooa," said Luther.

The cowgirl whirled. Lovely and contemptuous, she looked down at us. "Do your mothers know where you are?" She turned again and her wonderful ass swept away.

"Get up," I said. "Come on, loudmouth, get up. Jesus, couldn't you just keep quiet for a minute?"

"She liked it," he said. "They like it when you tell 'em they look good."

Luther's company would wear at you. Before long we were outside a corral and he was throwing dirt clods at milling, saucer-eyed horses. He wouldn't be restrained. "You're worthless," I told him. "You're the dumbest sonofabitch I ever met." And I left him there.

I circled around to the calf chutes. The creak of saddle leather, ropers with pigging strings in their teeth. Sad bleating. I liked the commotion but found myself developing wrong sympathies for the calves. I wandered off into a section of the parking lot where I thought I heard firecrackers. From a tall stand of weeds came my name. "Pete." It was Ernie, a Camel hanging from a corner of his mouth and half his face closed against the curling smoke. He was working resin into an old bull rope. He looked good to me, competent. He looked like he belonged right where he was. "Where you been?" he asked me. I described my morning to him. "That's Luther," he said. "You should've kicked his ass."

"He gets it kicked all the time. Doesn't do him any good."

"You know what's comin' up?" Pete asked me. "Steer ridin'. I wanted to get on a bull, but they said I had to wait a year. You wanna ride?"

"I haven't got the entry fee," I said.

"For steer ridin'? You don't gotta pay money to make a fool outta yourself. It's a kid thing."

"Then I'll leave it to the kids."

"Yeah, but it's good practice."

Practice for something I never intended to do. But I

said, "I'll try anything once. Long as it isn't those little teeny ones. It'd just be mean to get on one of them."

Ernie told me that the rodeo committee had been unable to afford an announcer that year and that the announcer's stand was where we should be. Best seat in the house. The bucking chutes were right below us. We could hear bulls snorting, sudden reports from hoof and horn, the flat clank of cowbells, and the riders talking fast and high: "Get him squared around, come on now, get him . . . prod him, would you?" Then things would be quiet for a second and they'd blow out of the chute. Most of the cowboys were making their eight-second rides. It didn't look easy, but it didn't look impossible either.

"That bull's one of my dad's," Ernie said of a fairly small Angus. "See that guy, havin' to spur him? You ever see a bull rider do that before? It's ridiculous. Crowhoppers. This ain't rodeo stock. They wanna have a rodeo, they oughta go out and get a real stock contractor."

A gray Brahma came out next. One jump. He planted his forelegs, pulled his rump around in a tight, lifting arc, and slammed the man aboard him into an edge of the gate. The man got up, retrieved his hat, and spit teeth into his cupped hand.

"If I'm gonna do this," I said, "I gotta take a leak."

We went back out into the parking lot, behind the Evans' truck. "We'll be on a lot smaller animals," Ernie told me. "But they'll be quicker, too. You can't let 'em get ahead of you."

"Whaddaya mean?"

"I mean, you better hang on."

"What do you say? You say 'outside,' or 'let me have him'?"

"I just nod my head at the gate man," Ernie told me. He could see that I was scared, and he was happy about it. So I pissed on his boots. He pissed on my penny loafers.

Eight of us gathered behind the chutes to ride. Ernie and I were the oldest of the bunch. My stomach hurt a little. I could see where I might get hurt, or worse, be made to look bad. An old cowboy took charge of us; the man was twisted up like an extension cord. He singled Ernie out and said, "You got a riggin', boy, so I guess that makes you first." To me the cowboy said, "You go down to that stock pen and run some of them yearlings up here. We gotta have somethin' to fit these littler fellas."

I hadn't been in the stock pen thirty seconds before I was kicked in the shin. By the time I cornered the calf that had kicked me, and punished it, Ernie had already made his ride. When I got back to the chutes, he was nowhere around. The cowboy running the show told me, "You're next."

"I don't have a rope," I said.

"You just get in there, son. We'll fix you up."

"This is the right size?" I asked him.

"This poor little thing is just a two-year-old. He'd still be good eatin' if they'd butcher him."

I climbed down onto the big brindle steer. It pinned my leg against the planking. The chute was built for horses and bulls. There was a lot of room for a steer to maneuver inside it. The cowboy leaned down over me. He had a plug of chew in his mouth that had been in there long enough to ferment. He looped a bull rope under the steer's belly and I set my hand under it. The cowboy cinched the rigging until I felt my fingers start to go numb. He grabbed my belt and slid me forward until my crotch was right up against the back of my hand. He breathed on me again and said, "Give 'er hell, kid." The gate flew open.

The steer, bunching and twisting beneath me. The shock to my shoulder. A shoe came off, the arena spun around us, and I was no longer afraid. Too busy for that, too well lit. A long string of slobber swung back from the brindle's nose, onto my face. The whistle blew. Just for show, I hung on for a few more jumps. Then I relaxed my grip. Only three and a half feet to the ground, but I hit it hard. Got up stunned and pleased with myself.

And looking for Ernie. We would strut together, I thought. We would make ourselves available to be admired by the cautious. I saw him at the far end of the arena, perched on the top rail. When I started toward him, he jumped down off the fence. Jumped down on the other side and went away somewhere.

There was a dance that night at the Grange Hall. I showed up without a fresh change of clothes, proud of every stain. Tired and giddy. The walls of the hall were hung with oppressive slogans concerning American agriculture--"Industry, Thrift, Our Bright Future" --and the music, I soon discovered, would consist of only two records. I had spotted Violet Quatayah the minute I walked in the door; she was among a faction of girls elaborately indifferent to my side of the room. Archie Bell and the Drells played "The Tighten Up"; the Beatles sang "Michelle." "Tighten Up," "Michelle," "Tighten Up," "Michelle." I had only so long to fix my courage. I crossed the floor, approached, waited, touched Violet's elbow. "Wanna dance?"

"Right now?"

"Well . . ."

"Come on," she said. She took my hand and led me to a clear space. We faced each other. She wore rouge and the translucent lipstick popular at that time. Her lips were set in a way I imagined to be sensuous. The fact that we were dancing was not reason enough for her to look at me. Violet knew one step and she repeated it with a terrifying kind of self assurance. I knew no steps, but I kept moving. When the song ended I thanked her and went outside for some air.

Predictably enough, Luther Pablo was sprawled in the front seat of his mother's car, drinking beer. We ignored the things I'd called him that morning and shared part of a warm six pack. He told me that since I'd last seen him, he'd ridden a Triumph 500, sassed the town sheriff, and learned that his cousin Adele had the clap. I countered with the merely factual story of Ernie and I at the rodeo.

Luther said that Ernie could now be found behind one of the two-holers. His tone implied that the mighty had rightfully fallen. "Dennis Knowsmuch bought him a pint of Seagrams. Just wasted him. He don't hold his liquor too good."

"He drank it all himself?"

"Practically chugged it," Luther said.

"I gotta see this."

We found him face down between the outhouses. Motionless. "Don't touch him," Luther said. "You don't wanna get your fingerprints on him--in case he's dead."

Ernie raised his head. It bobbled like a baby's. Weakly, he retched.

"Ernie, it's Pete. We're gonna get you away from these shitters. This'd make anybody sick." I started to lift him, and he swung on me. I dropped him. "Take it easy," I said.

"Leave me alone."

"Can't do it, Ernie. Somebody'll step on you if we leave you here." He got his legs under him, one at a time, and lurched off toward a barley field. Luther and I followed a while, but Ernie made it clear that all he wanted was away from us, that we weren't about to do him any good. "To hell with him," I said.

"Made him crazy, ain't it?"

"I'm goin' back in and dance, Luther."

"I would, too," Luther said, "but all them girls are too ugly for me."

I was a little surprised to find that Violet hadn't attached herself to anyone yet. She took note of my return to the hall. I tracked the tiny, furtive movements of her eyes, waited until the cycle of the two records came round to "Michelle," and then I asked her to dance again. The slow tune. The girl at the record player was kind enough to play it twice consecutively. Violet's gradual surrender. She let herself collapse a little in my grip, accepted my cheek against her own. Her hair was dense, and long enough to brush back and forth across my forearms. So much heat from so little friction. Violet rejected my next suggestion, but before we parted ways, she confessed, "I kind of like you. You're almost as neat as Jack."

I walked home that night with a very high opinion of myself. Brave, bighearted me. The certainty of that hour was that the world would surrender what I wanted from it.

My dad's voice carried up the stairs. "You didn't eat all those donuts, did you?"

"Hunh?" My quilt--lemon-colored in the early light, smothering.

"Aren't you up yet, Pete?"

"I'm up," I said.

"You damn well better be. You ate my breakfast."

I threw back the quilt to lie there, cool and naked. Outside my window, Main Street. It was covered with horse shit and meditative quiet. My legs seemed longer than I'd remembered them. I was gaining, I thought, gaining a little in all my parts. I dressed and went downstairs. The floor, sticky underfoot; our one spitoon, overturned. Dad was in the kitchen. "Quite the mess, huh?"

"These people are pigs," I said.

"You're talkin' about the folks that pay our rent. Everybody's got a right to get sloppy now and again." A sweet-tempered man, my father. If we hadn't looked so much alike, I'm sure no one would have ever believed I was flesh of his flesh.

"I'll do the pancakes," I said. "I was the one that ate the donuts."

"That'd be fair, but I never did learn to like 'em black."

We were sitting at the bar, eating our breakfast, when Arthur Roedeker came in. Arthur sat down a few stools away from us, folded his hands in front of him. He lived on Social Security and never a penny of it passed through our till. Dad nudged me. "Arthur," I said, "you want some pancakes?" It looked like my question had gone past him, like he was considering a vanishing point just beyond his knuckles. After a bit, he said, "Quieted down some today, ain't she, Gus?"

"Yeah," Dad said. "I make my nut on rodeo weekend, but they about wear a guy out. I'm ready to do some fishin'."

Arthur looked me up and down. We didn't like each other. "Too late for pancakes," he said. "If I was wantin' to eat, it'd be lunch."

Word had it that Arthur Roedeker had cut a wide swath in his day, and I'd heard the stories. But the only Arthur I knew lived in a tourist cabin and came around all liver-spotted to trade on my Dad's generosity. And he often came around early. That, more than anything else, turned me against him. I won't say that swamping the Oasis was ever quite delightful. Under certain conditions, though, the routine could offer its small compensations. Dark as a cave. Beer signs sparkling here and there, fake waterfalls pouring endlessly through ideal landscapes. When just the two of us were there, Dad would turn on the jukebox and sing with it. He could sing like Ray Price, sing like Red Sovine, sing like the angels, I imagine, if they'd ever recorded anything. But if someone else was there, he'd turn shy. With Arthur sitting at the bar, I was especially aware of my work as drudgery.

An hour later, when Ernie showed up, I felt like I'd been found out; not so good to have him see me wearing rubber gloves, using a mop. It was not, I thought, very manly equipment. But Ernie had beaten the swagger out of himself that morning. His Resistol had not lived up to its brand name. The crown was crushed, the brim drooping all around.

"You look like you been run through a wringer," I said.

"Went drinkin' with Dennis Knowsmuch. Ooh, oonh . . . what you got in that bucket? Gawd, that's awful."

I knew somehow that he remembered seeing me the night before and that he was going to pretend he didn't.

For some reason I liked the narrow and definite outline of Ernie's pride, a boundary I respected even at the expense of my curiosity. I mentioned that I'd been to the dance and let it go at that.

"What do we do next?" he asked me. He'd been trained to earn his way.

We mucked out the bathrooms. Here Ernie was heroic, his craw convulsing at every foulness we encountered. I had him brush down the felt on the pool table. We carried beer from the walk-in cooler to the refrigerated shelves behind the bar. The work raised a cold sweat on him. He claimed it was good for him. When we had almost finished, Arthur Roedeker shifted on his stool, leaned over his free coffee and said, "I seen you ride yesterday, Ernie. How come you never made the whistle?"

"Steer was tryin' to put me into the fence. I jumped off." It cost him something to say this.

"First time I've known an Evans to worry about the fence," Arthur said. "I seen your brother Marvin, one time up in Arlee--bronc pitched him into a storm fence, and he never quit grinnin'."

"Yeah," I said, "cause Marvin is an idiot."

Then, for maybe a minute, nobody said anything. I could feel my jaw muscles working, my dad's eyes on me. "Pete," he said, "I wish you'd learn to watch that mouth of yours." He threw me the keys to the car. "You boys take off now. Blow the stink off, get some fresh air."

"We're not finished yet," I said.

"Get your swimmin' gear and take off," he said, and he grinned at us.

The heat of the day closed around us like a big hand. We had no choice but to leave the windows open. Grit from the road furred my teeth. Ernie pulled his Camels from his boot, lit one, took a couple drags and threw it out. He sighed and threw the rest of the pack out. "It's about time to be gettin' in shape," he said. Two-a-day football practices were a week away. Ernie weighed about a hundred and thirty pounds but had every reason to expect he'd be a brilliant scatback in the coming season. He had instincts. He moved like a land crab.

"Are you gonna be in trouble?" I asked him. He didn't know.

"I don't see why you couldn't go swimmin'," I said. "Long as they're gonna give you a hard time anyway. Might as well put it off as long as you can."

"They'll be wonderin' about me," he said.

We turned off the county road and onto the Evans' lane which cut through their lower pasture, a forty-acre field covered with five acres worth of Johnson grass. Royce Evans bred his mares to an Arabian stud and the products of these unions were all around us. To me, they looked underfed. Long-barreled beauties, bent to the earth. These horses were the source of most of the Evans' income. They had a reputation for being fast, durable, and spirited, but they weren't recognized by any breeding association. And they weren't treated like pets. Royce expected what was his to survive neglect.

The house and all the outbuildings had been against the weather without paint or oiling for twenty years; they had turned gray. Nailed to a wall of the pump-house was a coyote carcass--I'd been told it was a coyote--by then it was a piece of curled gristle. The

Evans' one stab at decoration.

We pulled up in front of the house and got out of the car. Royce was sitting on the porch, braiding the handle of a quirt. As we walked up to him, he looked at us without lifting his face away from his work. Just cut his eyes. We stopped. "Runnin' around bucknaked--that the style now, Pete?" I was in my swimming trunks. I explained that I was going to the river. He'd made me feel stupid. Royce rarely failed to make me feel stupid. He asked his son, "What happened to you?"

"I stayed in town last night."

"No shit. Sam had to do your milkin' for you."

"I've done his chores for him. A lot of times."

"You stay with him?"

"Pete's just givin' me a ride home. I got drunk. Slept in the Post Office."

"Like a bum."

"Yeah, like a bum," Ernie said. "And now I'm goin' back in and go swimmin'. Might even stay the night again."

"I could give a good goddamn what you do, boy."

"Wait here," Ernie told me. "I'll get my trunks." He went into the house and I heard his mother yelling at him, Ernie yelling back.

Royce heard it, too. "So," he said, "I guess you're some kind of cowboy now, huh, Pete?" It was like an accusation.

"Ernie's the cowboy."

"No. No, I don't think he's got much taste for it." The strands of leather moved in his hands.

"He's . . ." Royce's eyes turned to me again. I went back to the car and waited for Ernie.

I drove fast on the way back into town, made the tires

sling gravel at every corner. We were the only thing moving through the countryside and all around us, it seemed, time had wound down and stopped. Ernie wouldn't talk, wouldn't look at me. Kept his face turned to the window. There was a thick sworl of freckles on the back of his neck. "People get strange ideas," I told him. "They'll make a big deal outta nothin'."

"What're you talkin' about?"

"You jumped off a steer. So what?"

"Why'd you have to bring that up? I wasn't even thinkin' about that."

"It's no big deal," I said.

"You hang on as long as you can. That's the whole idea of it. You hung on, and you're not even . . . You hung on."

"I didn't have any reason not to," I told him. "Nobody wants to get bunged up, that's just natural."

"You know all about natural, do you?"

"I know when to bail out," I said. "That's how I keep so handsome."

We bought Cokes at the Mercantile and drove out to a place where there were rocks to shield us from the Laughing Man's current. We met little Billy Johnson, climbing up out of the swimming hole. "Gimme a ride back to my house," he said.

"We just got here," I said. He was carrying swim fins, two feet of toy boat, and something big made of styrofoam, but he hadn't thought to wear any shoes. "How's that water?" I asked him. He was bright red, and it wasn't sunburn. His lips were blue.

"It's nice," he said.

And, if you worked it right, it was. Ernie and I would lay on the rocks until we were sweating, then dive, then scramble right back out. This was a way to make yourself tingle. We listened to the sound the water made, wrapping around the outcropping. Ernie regretted throwing his cigarettes away. "This is the best hangover cure goin'," he said. "I think I'm even gettin' hungry." He pulled his knees up to his chest, rested his chin on them, and stared across the river. I was afraid he was going to turn thoughtful.

"I like to eat four times a day," I said. "And, so far, I've only ate once. If I'm not careful, I start wastin' away."

"You got a nice guy for an old man," he said.

"We can charge hamburgers at the Y," I said.

"You know that?"

"He's a nice guy," I said.

We lay on the rocks. Middle of a ten-hour afternoon. My eyes grew heavy but never quite closed. Two hundred yards downstream, the bridge. Trusses taller than anything else in town--there was something hopeful and inviting about the way they were cast against the near horizon. It was like someone had written a word there in a language I could understand but not pronounce. "You ever see anybody jump off that bridge, Ernie?"

"Lots of 'em."

"No, I mean the top part."

"I . . . Far as I know, nobody's jumped from there. You mean the tippy-top?"

"I wonder why not?"

"Cause it's . . ." Ernie pulled on his boots. "Let's take a look at it," he said. And off he went. Following behind him, I was reminded of a girl walking in new high heels. Naked legs and clackety-clack. We climbed up the bank, walked down the road to the bridge.

"Why's this river so cold, Ernie?"

"Cause it comes out of the mountains. It's melted snow."

"They all do. The Flathead, the Little Bitter Root. But they're warm. By this time of year, those other ones are warm."

"Well, you got me. Why you wanna know, anyway? What difference does it make?"

"I wanna know everything," I told him. "Don't you?"

"Remember that story Mrs. Ashcraft read us?"

"I'm gonna remember from the fourth grade?"

"It was about a kid who wanted to know everything," Ernie said. "It fucked him up. You're not supposed to know everything. It's bad."

"Far as Mrs. Ashcraft was concerned, everything was bad."

We walked the length of the bridge, looking down over the railing at the water. Looking for depth. In the middle, right where the superstructure arched highest, there was a patch of darkness. "I bet it's fifteen, twenty feet deep down there," I said.

"There's no way of tellin', though."

I looked up. "It'd be . . . it'd really get your blood runnin', wouldn't it?"

"Looks pretty shallow to me," Ernie said.

"I'll curve when I go in."

"You gonna do it?"

"I feel good, Ernie."

"You gonna do it?"

"Yeah."

"From the top?"

"If I keep feelin' good. Won't know till I get up there."

"All right, " he said. He pulled his boots off.

"This is just me, Ernie. Nothin' says you gotta . . ."

"If you can do it, I can."

"That's not the . . ."

He swung onto the latticework of the nearest upright. I let him put a little distance between us and started up after him. The steel was hot so we moved fast.

We were fifty feet off the water with ten feet left to climb when Ted Norbertson, the high school math teacher, drove up on the bridge below us. He stopped his car, got out, and started yelling at us. "Hey. Hey, you two." He looked small. I liked that. Small and frantic. I liked what we had done to him. "Get down off there," he said. Red-headed Ted, his arm swinging helplessly toward our place in the sky.

Ernie stopped and looked down at me. "You think this is all right?"

"I'm jumpin'," I said.

He started to climb again, headed for the tippy-top.

2.

The pain was brilliant where the river slapped the undersides of my arms. The shock of the cold--melted snow. I hit bottom and felt bone push through the top of my foot, a keening pressure in my ears. Vertigo. I looked up through the water at a butter-yellow sun, kicked, kicked again, and broke surface thirty yards downstream from the bridge. "Ernie?"

I treaded water. It was so clean around me. No scum, no chop--nothing. Wouldn't have know it was moving if the bank hadn't been sliding by. "Ernie?" I paddled in circles. Two slow circles. "Err-niiie?" I dived. Couldn't see a thing, couldn't hold my breath for long--there was no good reason to try. The bridge was receding. Senselessly, I swam toward it, making no headway at all against the current. I dived again, dived until the backs of my legs started cramping. I drifted to a bend in the river where I was able to steer myself to the bank without having to swim much. I crawled out and onto a hot brown sandbar.

A few minutes later Ted Norbertson's Studebaker turned off the river road and came toward me over the rocks, his motor pulling hard against first gear. He got out. His clothes were wet up to his chest.

"Where's Ernie?"

"I don't know," he said.

"Where is he?"

"I told you, I don't know. He didn't come up."

"Find him. You gotta find him."

"We'll find him. But . . . Look at you. I told you to get down. I know you heard me."

"He didn't come up?"

"Not yet."

"You gotta . . ."

"Shut up," he said. He got behind me and pulled me to my feet. My weight rocked onto the bad one. "Hurts, huh, Pete? That's just too bad, isn't it?"

At the hospital, a doctor plastered me from mid thigh to toes in an L-shaped cast. "See how much goop we use for one little broken bone?" he said. "That's all there was--about the size of your little finger. You won't be able to break this cast, young man, and I bent it so you won't be able to put your foot to the ground. If you can keep it dry for six weeks, we'll see about a walking-cast."

After they'd made my dad leave, I spent the night making the nurses do for me. I lay in crisp sheets and buzzed every half hour for more fruit juice. The rustle of their uniforms, gently marking time, the cool confidence of their voices, saying, "Sleep. You need your sleep."

Very little pain. My life moved inside me, a separate, callow force and no amount of pills or soothing would make it rest.

I was in the cargo part of the Pontiac. "I'll wash it," I said. "I'll wash it when we get home."

"How you gonna do that?"

"I just will. We only went out to Ernie's and back."

"That's twelve miles on county road." Dad made a palm print in the seat beside him.

"It did get dusty," I admitted.

"That's what I don't like about a station wagon--the way they leak dust . . . But it don't matter. What good's a car if you can't drive it where you wanna go?"

"I . . ."

"They're made to be drove," he told me.

The Oasis did no business that day, though it was open. From my room I heard Dad running the buffer over the floor. He brought me sandwiches. The afternoon passed. He brought me soup for supper. "You don't have to wait on me," I said.

"You're supposed to take it easy for a while."

"I feel fine," I told him. "I better figure out how to use these crutches."

"Yeah, well . . . I just put three layers of wax on the floor down there. Could be slick. If I'd been thinkin' about what I was doin' . . ."

"Dad--did they say what he looked like?"

"When they found him?"

"I shouldn't wanna know?"

"Coroner said his neck was broke. He couldn't say how it happened." A glass of milk in his hands. It had been years since I'd touched the stuff, but he'd brought me a glass of milk. He drank it for me and licked it from his lips. "Royce called. He wants to drop by and see you."

"About what?"

"I didn't ask him, Pete. He's got the right."

"What'll I tell him?"

"I don't know. Depends on what he wants to find out."

"He's comin' tonight?"

"Waitin' won't make it easier."

He was right about that much. It was eleven-thirty and the neon sign on our roof was buzzing like a big insect before Royce finally came. He was a small man. Coming up the stairs, he was barely heavy enough to make them squeak. He leaned into the room, entirely clean shaven. "Mind if I come in a minute?" The first time I'd heard him ask for anything.

"Sure, Mr. Evans. Sorry about the way it smells in here. It's been a while since I did my laundry."

He stood over me, his hands clasped behind his back, his lips pursed, and I had the terrible sense, as I always did with Royce, that he understood me perfectly. My mouth moved, dry sounds came out. Royce went to my dresser and leafed through a geography text I'd stolen from school. "This Lapland looks like quite the place," he said. "My hat's off to anybody who can herd reindeer."

"He was a good kid, Mr. Evans."

Royce turned to me. He moved slow so I wouldn't flinch. "I'm glad he had somebody to buddy up with. That's . . . He thought you . . . I don't know. He thought you were all right."

"He was the best friend I had."

"I never knew what was goin' on with him," Royce said. "I don't guess I tried very hard, either." He pulled the curtain back from my window. I could tell that he was tired of looking at me; I was tired of being looked at.

"Any boy worth his salt is gonna raise a little hell, Pete. Sometimes it just works out bad." Grief hadn't changed him. I saw that his sorrow was not as fresh as the death of his son, that there was something sad always waiting in Royce, waiting for new reasons. "You'll be welcome out at the place," he said. "There's a deal after the funeral and . . . You're still welcome at our place any time."

As is the case with many worthless persons, Luther made a faithful pal. He was my first social visitor. I lay amid the cellophane leavings of several meals when he came. "What you been doin'?" he asked me.

"Restin'," I said.

"You tired?"

"No."

"They give you some pills?" he asked. "The brown kind?"

Mine were red and white. "Contains codeine," I read from the bottle. "Is that good?"

"They screwed up, man. They gave you cough medicine. That's what's in cough medicine."

"I had a compound fracture," I told him because I liked the sound of it.

"You're lucky. When I broke my arm, it was a whipback fracture. They're the worst." He'd spent part of his life in Fresno, California. Anything that happened to anyone we knew had already happened more lavishly to Luther in Fresno. "You lucked out," he said. "You got outta football this year."

"I didn't want to get out of it."

"But you're no good. It's no fun if you ain't good."

"I gained twenty-five pounds since last year."

"I gained thirty," said Luther. And then he put on what he must have thought was a serious expression and he asked me, "What about Ernie?"

"What about him?"

Luther got up and made a few turns around the room on my crutches. "Well he's . . . you know. Pretty rough deal. I almost died once, myself. I never told you about that time I was in a coma? Don't laugh, man, it ain't funny."

"I'm not laughin' at you, Luther. I'm laughin' with you. You're all right."

"I am now, but you should've seen me then. Woke up and my head was all shaved. But at least I got to see Jesus. He was a lot nicer than they say."

I asked Dad about the higher purpose the priest had spoken of. What was it? He didn't know. I asked him about the custom of sending flowers to the dead, when they couldn't enjoy them. That was also beyond his understanding. I wanted to know why were we supposed to drive with our lights on. "This is just the routine," he said. "It's a way they've worked out to make people feel better."

"I don't feel any better. Does this stuff make you feel better?"

He shrugged.

"Did you see the way they were all lookin' at me in the church?"

"Nobody was lookin' at you," he said.

But they had been. We'd sat together in the back pew, me remembering how I'd made fun of Ernie the day he'd come to school with ash on his forehead, Dad crimping the cover of a hymnal with his thumb. They'd been looking at us; almost everyone we knew was there.

"Boy," I said. "This is a tiny little town. A thing like this gets remembered."

The caravan of mourners turned onto the cemetery road and started parking along it. People got out of their cars, formed in small groups, and walked in to the grave. It wasn't far from the road.

"You don't have to get out," he said. "They wouldn't expect you to."

Against the poor fields around it, the cemetery was an unlikely shade of green. The crowd formed a semicircle. Melanie Prysock's little girl squirmed out of her mother's arms and made a short run for freedom, shrieking happily. Her pink legs continued to churn after she'd been caught.

"I wonder what they think they're puttin' in the ground," I said.

"Me, I'm selfish. All I can think about is how glad I am it wasn't you."

"I am, too. Glad. But . . . Dad, I kind of wish I wasn't. I should feel worse than I do."

Around the grave they joined in prayer.

"It'll get worse before it gets better," my father told me. "You got away with it--he didn't. Just stupid, both of you, but you got away with it. And when you're an old man, there'll still be days when you catch yourself wonderin', 'Why him?' You'll never come up with the answer. But, goddamnit, you're here and . . . you're here, you know what I mean?"

I knew. I felt like I'd been let loose in the wind.

PUNTA COYOTE

Babies and a piglet made restive night sounds aboard a second class bus bound from Cabo San Lucas to Tijuana, and Katy Barnett, seated well to the rear of the airless coach with mescal dripping warm and unavoidable from the luggage rack onto her lap, wondered, How do these people sleep? Sagging bodies enclosed her. Shame mingled with a loathing she had begun to conceive for those more practiced in their misery. From somewhere near at hand, what she took to be love songs issued through a cracked speaker, forlorn for hours, at all tempos.

According to her guidebook, the Chinese had come to Baja as traders, the French to mine copper, mestizos to do what they had always done on the mainland, farm and raise children in the bosom of the church. The Barnetts were there because Katy had waged a long campaign against the cloying comfort and familiarity of their life together. We've got to do something, she had said around the time of their twentieth anniversary. Anything.

A romantic anomaly on the map of North America, the Sea of Cortez was once again in view, gliding along beside her in the window. Quicksilver. Katy remembered italicized references from her guidebook that mentioned lost tribes, caches of bone waiting to powder at your touch. And sharpened stone artifacts. Hanging arid and profuse in the skies around Loreto, the stars suggested hoarfrost. Gently she set her hand on her husband's knee. Just as gently, she removed it.

Since they had come south on this road, the few conversations the Barnetts had managed, apart from spidery discussions between themselves, had all worked around to the subject of Highway 1. A young man from Milwaukee whose mottled flesh was better suited to his home latitude told them one night in a bar that ". . . it's just twelve hundred miles of ugly-ass blacktop. They can get the big refrigerator trucks down here now, and that's all right, I guess. Truck in frozen orange juice. But I liked it better when a guy could come down here and get completely away from those Coupe de fucking Villes." There was an unmistakable wistfulness about all the people the Barnetts had met here, always the implication that this had been a better place before the advent of tourists like themselves--before the road was paved. Still, it was just as well, Katy thought, that there was at least a line of asphalt available to the headlights. Highway 1 was awash in sand drifts, and had been at intervals, for miles, the bus bursting along through them like an overland speedboat. The drip from the luggage rack slowed, stopped. Her pants dried quickly, but smelled then as if she had been urinating in them.

The sun rose over Bahia Fertilidad.

In the seat across from Katy's, and wedged in the aisle between them, there was a family of four. As the waters of the bay shaded through steel to royal blue, Katy heard the woman, in fact it was just within the threshold of her hearing, murmuring to her sons, her husband, "Tst . . . Mardo . . . tsst. Ruben. Viejo." The woman's two sons had slept standing and when she roused them their weight withdrew from Katy's shoulder. A luxury. Katy envied the reverence of the whispers that passed between this family. Similar intimacies rippled through the seats around them. An odor of humanity was swelling, too, becoming more complex. Katy could neither ignore nor accustom herself to her own rich contribution. She would have liked to ask the old woman how she achieved so much authority, so much tenderness, and what, if anything, the embroidery on those shirt fronts meant. From the very corner of her left eye Katy saw that the elder, or at least the larger of the two boys was fingering her hair. The broad boy who had answered to "Mardo."

Katy forced herself to look up. What to say? In any language? She thought that it might be best to be a little afraid, but the boy was so tender, so smooth of face and obviously witless.

"Art. Art, wake up." The hand withdrew from the blurred margin of her vision. Her husband jerked, opened his eyes. He took stock of his surroundings and sucked a quantity of air through gritted teeth. Worn and in profile like this, he was cut too spare, only the nose and Adam's apple generously formed; he suggested far more hardship than he had ever known. He turned partly toward her and winced. "Where are we?"

"Still a long way from Tijuana, that's all I know. I wish we could pry one of these windows open."

"Well, we can't," he said. "If we ever go anywhere again, we're flying." Art's head began a mechanical traverse, fifteen degrees to the left, fifteen to the right.

He moved gingerly, his eyes glazed with concentration, and when he'd made himself adequately supple again, he studied a phrase book. "'Where is the museum?' 'Is your aunt from Barcelona?' You have to wonder how they dreamed this stuff up. 'When will your sister arrive?' I guess it never occurred to these people that you might just want to ask someone where the hell you're at." On an impulse he tugged at Ruben's sleeve. Ruben, with a forelock like a crow's wing. Mardo's brother. "Excuse me," Art said. "Ehm . . . excuse me. Eh . . . donde . . . eh . . . es . . ." He had Ruben's full attention. The whole family, with the exception of Mardo, attentive; all of them, again excepting Mardo, handsome, waiting for clarification.

"What are you asking them, Art?"

"I'm just trying to find out where we are."

"Look out the window, Honey. We're nowhere."

Art thrust the index finger of his left hand into the air and said, "Nosotros . . . ?" He brought the index finger of his right hand together with its mate so that they aimed toward heaven as do children's in the church-steeple-people game. "Un-see-you-dad?" he asked hopefully.

The family was stunned for a moment. Katy could tell that they wanted very much to be helpful. The patriarch, pressed to the far wall of the bus behind his wife and children, finally collected himself enough to introduce them all as the Avellanos.

"Señor Avellanos," Art acknowledged. "Donde?"

Señor Avellanos, confused, offered an answer that was long, lyrical, and likely diplomatic. But of no use. Ruben joined in; it was clearly a complicated matter. Soon Señora Avellano was correcting them both. They began to laugh softly among themselves, and the

Barnetts, none the wiser, were forgotten. Art speculated on their progress, the lay of the land.

The Baja peninsula is a continental afterthought; buff and russet cordilleras twist down its length, evidence of a convulsive tectonic birth. Between two of these ranges several small springs result in a river, just ten miles of river bearing a half dozen names and emptying at the mouth of Bahia Fertilidad. Along its banks flourish some thousand acres of date palms, and, less conspicuously, the village Proviso. Here the Avellanos nodded courteously to the gringos of their recent acquaintance and left the bus. At Katy's insistence, --"See, Art? Didn't you see it when we went over the bridge? There's a village down there"--the Barnetts also got off. Their driver climbed to the roof of the coach, climbed it for the second time this stop, to throw down their luggage and invective. Then, without another word or glance in their direction, he was back in the driver's seat, pulling away from them as fast as the first few gears of his transmission would permit.

"Boy," Art said despondently.

Already the Avellanos were considerably above them, moving in single file up a street that was about to turn path and lead through a crease in the hills. Katy picked up her suitcase, her shoulder bag. They were very heavy. "Come on," she said, "we have to go down the hill." Three grinning curs loped in sideways to accompany them. A small girl holding a baby on cocked hip stared at them in dim disbelief from the side of the road, both children host to clusters of thirsty gnats along the rims of their eyelids. The Barnetts descended through a neighborhood of wattle and thatch into a better part of the village where the occasional freshet channeled upriver from the bay. Dreamy.

"Sleepwalking," Katy recalled, was a word she had used to goad Art into making this trip.

Soldiers or police or sailors-at-arms loitered against the wall of a barracks. Merchants and housewives swept, then made mud of the dust in the streets with hoses and canvas buckets. A block from the plaza stood a bright new PeMex station, across from that a bank wrapped partly in smoked plate glass, otherwise Proviso was much as it had been in 1847. In 1847 its hastily assembled militia had repelled a boatload of American marines, the event being celebrated on the day of the Barnett's arrival. "Not exactly a tourist trap," Art said.

In sun-bleached pastel lettering, two buildings represented themselves as hotels. At the first, a man with a guitar gravely nodded "no" before Katy could finish framing her question about a room. As a formality the man slipped into his sandals and set aside his guitar, but he had no accommodation for them. The same was true, as they learned on the strength of an adolescent's shrug, at the Hotel Moderno.

So sensibly made and reasonably priced on Sear's shelves only a month ago, their plaid luggage now weighed like real wealth as they carried it through a small grid of streets, watched. "We could sit in the square," Katy said.

A woman leaned through a Dutch door, smiling. It was an easy smile constructed of precious metals set in blued teeth. "Helados?" she asked them. She swung open the lower half of the door and beckoned to them. Agreeably mystified, the Barnetts entered a room where one fan swung paddle-bladed from the ceiling and another hummed on a shelf. The woman rounded a counter to open a chest containing three gallon tubs.

"Vainilla? Aquacate? Dátil?" Wraiths of chilled air floated in the chest.

"Ice cream," sighed Katy.

Ceramic bowls, chilled spoons, a smooth collusion of crystal and cream. "I'm going to try every flavor she's got," Katy said. "This is hand-cranked, that's the only way you can make it come out like this." The woman behind the counter continued to smile at them. Katy's shirt clung to her, absorbing the cool turbulence of the room.

"I guess you know what comes next," Art said. "We go up and sit beside that road until another bus comes along. Could be another couple of hours--maybe another day or two. Who knows? In this country? What if the Virgin had a birthday, or some saint? They might shut the whole place down over a thing like that. Do you know what it's going to be like up there?" His voice rose by quarter-octave stages. Her husband bore anxiety poorly.

"There's only one road, Art. I can't imagine we won't be able to find some way out of here."

"Do you know what the top of my head's going to look like? This was a mistake. In this country, getting off anything that's pointed north and still moving is a mistake."

"Well, I'm sorry," Katy said.

"It's not your fault."

"I was the one who wanted to get off the bus," she said. "If it's not my fault, whose fault would it be?"

"What else? Now, I guess we've got to get in an argument, too."

A tall man came into the shop, cradling a parfait glass like a chalice in his long fingers. He grinned weakly at them, then directed the good humor woman to fill his glass with layers of ice cream, nuts, sliced orange. "Más naranja," he told the woman. "Más, señora."

"The guy thinks he's a real connoisseur," Katy said.

The man turned to regard them. Waves of salty black hair lapped toward the crown of his head. His eyes were also quite dark, the irises seemingly afloat. Katy could tell they were under some kind of scrutiny by the way the man's lips were pursed. "California," he said. "Northern California."

"Sir?" Katy said.

"Doesn't take me long, does it? A few syllables and I've got you. Louis Uriarte." The immediate friend, he extended his hand, paused just long enough to let Art mention their names, then further introduced himself with a sorrowful account of his life to date. He was Colombian originally, but his mother had come from Wilkes-Barre, had been in fact, one of the Wilkes-Barre Smiths. He'd been disenfranchised from an excellent family, and his long suit, a vastly retentive memory, was skewering him. Where, he asked the Barnetts, might a man expect to find a little justice? He told them of an ex-wife living in the Zona Rosa, enjoying the fruits of a ridiculously generous divorce settlement and the company of some of Mexico City's more interesting diplomats. "And me. Look at me." His left foot was wrapped in a greasy bandage, his neck in something neither tie nor cravat but paisley. " . . . not a single competent barber, no place to buy cologne or decent candy. If I didn't have my radio . . ."

"You live here?" Katy asked him.

"For three and a half years, give or take a minute."

"We're from Illinois," Art said.

"Oh, but you picked up that California lilt

somewhere. I'm good with accents. Especially Americans'." His own accent was variable. "I spent the best part of my career with the Haas Brothers in Dayton," he said. "Finest department store in Ohio, or it was then. Managed their circular department for them. Married the damn secretary. This isn't Graciela, but another woman. Women. I also smoke like a fiend. Say, you wouldn't happen to have any recent newspapers with you? The rest of the planet could be in flames and we wouldn't know about it here."

A mile downriver from Proviso, on a plateau with a good view of the bay and of the sea to the north and the east, there was another hotel. Louis Uriarte was its manager. When he learned the Barnetts had need of him, his manner at once turned less desperate and more patronizing. Katy regretted the hick friendliness she and Art could not put away. Something about this Louis turned basic courtesies to straw in her mouth. An indifferent driver, he wheeled a springshot Ford Galaxy, pluming roseate dust. "We're selective about our guests," he explained as the road steepened near the top of the plateau. At the top they lurched in a patch of loose dirt and a hose pulled away from the radiator. They crested in steam, spraying rock. "The Excelsior," Louis announced.

It was a lonely arrangement of shell-white plaster and Spanish tile, a monolith but for a few second floor windows. Native desert prevailed right up to its walls, but just past the portico there grew from a flagstone courtyard a kind of domestic jungle, at least three tiers of greenery; some part of it, they were told, always in shade.

"Mr. Uriarte," Katy said. "It's beautiful."

"Please, that's Louis. Or Loo-eess, as we say it." He told them that, since they had come so unexpectedly, they should be prepared to wait a while for their room. "The cleaning woman," he said, "isn't always easy to find around this time of day." And then he disappeared. Left to themselves again, the Barnetts wilted, Katy in an oak rocker, Art along the wall of a planter, in a wayfarer's pose.

"This is about what I had in mind all along," he said.

The bed sagged beside her and Katy released a complicated sigh to let her husband know she was awake. Art turned on a nightstand lamp. "You should have seen yourself," he said, "sprawled out like a dishrag."

"I sure wasn't having any dreams." She swung out of bed, padded across the tile, pushed a pair of heavy shutters open; another moonless night coming on. "God, I slept all day. Did you get a nap?"

"Don't you think that's the last thing I need? This whole trip has been a nap for me."

Their suitcases were stacked on a closet shelf. Art said that he'd put her clothes in the bureau drawers. Katy moved to a dresser, brushed her hair in the mirror. Beveled glass, burled maple. A slight imperfection in the glass foreshortened and flattered her face and elongated Art's reflection. He was admiring her.

"This is a nice room," she said.

"Way better than nice, Katy. Notice these walls, how they're arched? I forget what they call that, but it's one of those touches builders can't be bothered with anymore."

"I suppose. But it smells like our attic in here. I

think it's been a while since they rented this out."

"This is the only room on the second floor with any furniture in it," Art said importantly. "I've been all through the place. Fireplaces in every room. How often do you suppose you'd light a fire down here? What would you burn? Elaborate, you know? Mosaics--everything." This was the kind of joy he brought home from meetings of the Craftsman's Guild. Sometimes it made her happy for him. "I wouldn't mind staying here a few days," he said.

"Here? No. I think I've had about enough of that Louis. I don't know why, but he kind of tires me out."

"Forget about Louis. He's not the main man around here. You hungry? We're invited for supper. I thought you might wear your nice dress." Art drew a line between the tips of his collar bones. "The one with the lace."

"It's wrinkled," she said. "And dirty."

Didn't matter. The evening before them was all promise as far as he was concerned. "You're going to see some new things," he told her. "I'vc got a surprise for you."

Louis waited in the courtyard. Upon their appearance at the top of the stair, he lit the candles on a card table draped in checked linen and set for four. He made them decline separate offers of gin and tonic, wine, scotch, bourbon, and a very unusual pilsener. He now acted like a boy among socially superior relatives. "These late night suppers are strictly Old World," he said. "Who wants to sleep on a full stomach these days?" Oily water did tricks with bouncing light in a bird bath. The table could almost be heard to whimper under the weight of the silver service.

Presently they were joined by a man whose age Katy placed at sixty, sixty-five years. Without a trace of his usual reticence with relative strangers, Art introduced the man as Señor Sean Maldonado, the Excelsior's owner. Maldonado held himself like one of those small dogs with broad faces, always braced for something. A little short of her own height. Barrel-chested. His mouth moved pink and most expressive within the wings of a white moustache. "I understand you've had an unpleasant trip, Mrs. Barnett. A shame. Beautiful women should not accept inconvenience." Over the diminished musculature of his arms, the skin hung like burlap. Katy was not, and had never been, beautiful. Not even pretty. Maldonado took her right hand, bowed as if to examine her fingertips, sat across the table from her. He looked at each of them in turn, reached a decision, and summoned a slouched attendant. "Miguelito. Agua para la mujer. Con limón."

"I hope Art hasn't given you the wrong impression, Mr. Maldonado. We've enjoyed your country. Most of the time."

"I had them drill a well through twenty meters of igneous rock," Maldonado said. "You'll never taste purer water."

"It was just that bus ride," Art said in a way that seemed to Katy pointlessly apologetic. "They kept letting people get on until nobody had room to move an inch one way or the other. Thing was hitting on maybe five cylinders. Thirty-five miles an hour for twelve hundred miles? Those people might still be on that thing. We had no idea there could be that much difference between first and second class."

Maldonado's eyes had not left Katy's face. "The

coincidence of my living here," he said, "inspires no patriotism in me. You may speak of the place any way you like."

"I happen to think Mexico is charming," Katy said with conviction but little basis in fact. "Among other things. A person should form more than one opinion, shouldn't they?"

"Charming, Mrs. Barnett?"

"Yes, Mr. Maldonado, charming."

His smile turned still more formal. It was clear that he considered one opinion enough.

"I don't know," Art said. "Summers aren't exactly mild where we're from, but we never expected something like what you've got down here. There's Baptists living on both sides of us back home. If they were here they'd think they'd died and gone to hell." He told of his skin's sensitivity to the sun, their half hour at a public beach, their motel in Cabo, " . . . a whole big group from one of the Cunard liners, so the prices were all out of sight. And the pool. They mixed it about half and half, chlorine and water. You couldn't get away from the smell. Swim in that, you'd come out blond every time. I guess we thought things would be more the way they used to be."

"How did things used to be?" Maldonado asked him.

"The way they were before they changed," Art said. Katy felt warmth rise in her cheeks. The kind of place, Art told them, where you wouldn't bother to shave more than once a week, where you wouldn't encounter chlorinated water or Nehi Grape Soda.

"And I suppose you were disappointed that there were no bandidos," Maldonado said.

"No, we're not that . . ." Art considered, deferred.

"Maybe we were, Sean, Maybe we were at that."

Sean? Katy saw nothing about the man to invite familiarity. He was still staring at her. "Change is illusory," Maldonado said. "You think Mexico is less than authentic because you happen to be seeing it in the last quarter of the twentieth century. Perhaps you saw all the antennae in Proviso? The place is ugly with them, I'll admit, but this country is now what it has always been . . ." His attention wandered. Antennae? Katy focused on the word. Parochial school Latin? She pictured a waist-high Maldonado under the tutelage of cruel nuns. Art prompted him with indications that he was about to be persuaded, so Maldonado finished his argument. "I've seen color television sets in huts with no provision for fresh water, no sanitation, no bedding, not so much as a mosquito net. Of course television could bring them the world, but it doesn't. Serves exactly as marijuana and cock fights did before it came. It's a sop for the senses. These people do not change. If they aren't born stupid, their culture demands that they find a way to make themselves stupid, and that has always been the case."

Miguelito, whose handsomely domed forehead suggested connection to the Maldonado line, served a chalky green broth. "This is unusual," Art said, obviously repulsed. "But delicious."

"Louis, go have Mrs. Yee tell you how the soup is made. I'm sure Mrs. Barnett can duplicate it for her husband."

"It's just turtle soup," Louis said sullenly, "not something they're likely to be serving . . ." He'd been sitting there in an attitude of stylized boredom, waiting it seemed for Maldonado to allow him into the conversation. Maldonado's chin swerved in the direction of the kitchen and Louis got up to limp away as commanded.

"Louis was somewhat inaccurate, Mrs. Barnett. The Excelsior is no longer a hotel, as such. But he felt that people of your quality should not be stranded in Proviso. Louis is often correct in matters like these. He thought I might enjoy your company--and I probably will. So he's thinking very well for himself today. Your husband has told you that I'd like you to stay as long as you possibly can? As my guests, of course."

"No, he hadn't told me that. Did you?"

"That was my surprise." Art wore a grin as stiff and colorful as a new shirt.

"Do I look like an innkeeper to you, Mrs. Barnett?" Maldonado asked her. "Do I look like a man to concern himself with whining tourists and the maintenance of thirty toilets?"

"Not exactly," Katy said.

When the food began to arrive in earnest, Miguelito ferrying camarones con ajo and hour-old tortillas and steaming baskets and pots to be left of necessity at their feet, Maldonado retired to a nearby hammock where he lit and kept relighting a missile-shaped cigar. He urged them through portions of meat sliced from hog, fish, and reptile, through gay heaps of salad and three different yellow fruits. "Eat everything," he told them, "or the staff will be offended." Dogged, almost without comment, they tried to comply. "You're perspiring so heavily," he told them, "because the blood has rushed from your head and extremities into your stomachs. That's exactly what we're trying to achieve. Satiation--still nothing quite so sedative, is there, as a full stomach? No, Louis, it is not uncomfortable. Short, shallow breaths, remember? If only you would get rid of that ridiculous scarf." Maldonado studied his Panatella with satisfaction and moved on to the subject of Bahia Fertilidad. They sank with him through phylum after subphylum, swam offshore through a crowded, cosmopolitan heaven. Their host claimed not to know the nomenclature for every little species, but the list he did know, which he recited, rolled on like high mass. He was bathed in the stark glow of a light fatal and attractive to flying insects; it cracked constantly as they surrendered themselves. Katy asked him if he hadn't traded one annoyance for another.

"Have you ever been to East Los Angeles, Mrs. Barnett?"

"We're not very well traveled."

"I wouldn't be concerned with that, if I were you. One place is as inhospitable as another. We're multinationals and we know, don't we Louis? Tell them about East Los Angeles."

"It's worse than Medellin," Louis said. "Worse than Caracas. And compared to a town like Dayton . . ."

"East Los Angeles is squalid, Mrs. Barnett. Nothing better or more interesting can be said of it. But I was comfortable there, just as I've been able to make myself comfortable here." Maldonado indicated the sizzling light, then Katy, a gesture that confused her completely. "Please don't mistake my offer for courtesy, Mrs. Barnett."

"Katy," Katy said.

"You should plan to stay for no less than a week--Katy."

She cited commitments: a son about to leave for his

sophomore year at Northwestern, her cat, the yard. ". . . first term is just around the corner now. Art's supposed to be back at school, varnishing desks by--what? Beginning of next week, isn't it?"

Maldonado drank broth from a mug. "If they hadn't been so forthright about it, Louis, would you have taken these people for teachers?--Yes, Mrs. Barnett, I've heard of your impending duties. Industrial Arts and Home Economics, wasn't that it? You must be very responsible people." From Maldonado, this sounded unlike flattery. "Remember," he said, "that it is also practical, and responsible, to accept opportunities as they present themselves." His legs scissored from the hammock. "I'm old," he said, and he went off to his apartment.

A motor stopped thrumming and the buglight snapped off.

"The generator," Louis explained. "Once Our Perfect Host goes to bed, the rest of us can stumble around in the dark."

"I can see where he wouldn't want to leave it running all night," Art said.

"Multinationals," Louis said with contempt. "One citizenship he doesn't hold is Mexican. You know who the owner of record is here? Yours truly. A sinecure, he calls it. I call it purgatory." He developed this theme at length.

Despite her rest earlier in the day, or possibly because of it, Katy fell asleep in her chair. Satiated. She woke some time later to find drool looped from lip to bodice, Louis gone, and Art lonely, glad of her company.

Morning here was no fresher than any other time of day. Dewless. Rust from the veranda's wrought iron railing smeared the sleeves of a sweater she hadn't needed to wear. Red on turquoise, a little like dawn. In order to have some time to herself, Katy had risen and crept from the room very early, but she soon recognized Maldonado's heels propped on the high side of his hammock's lopsided embrace. Though he couldn't see her, his presence forced a stillness, an instinct she did not understand. Delicious, in a way, the sense of being hidden.

Two campesinos came in through the portico and strode up to Maldonado like men of affairs. They wore huaraches and shapeless clothing. Briefly, musically, one of them spoke. Katy caught herself straining for the gist of Maldonado's reply. A soft, fast, Spanish sibilance in the atrium. The hammock was strung between two swooping date palms, and, every minute or so, another fruit would release from one of them to burst wet and sudden against the courtyard. Hat-in-hand, but not obsequious, Maldonado's associates would not allow themselves to flinch. The dates had reached this maturity overnight.

The door of the room Louis had told them was both his studio and living quarters opened to release a squinting tomcat, followed by Louis himself who, with expansive movements of his arms and a beatific look on his face, performed the pastoral drama, Taking the Morning Air; delighted to discover an audience, he shrilled up to Katy, "There she is."

At the sound of his voice, the campesinos turned toward him, pivoted, one of them reaching down inside his shirt. Louis held his hands up, palms out, shoulder high, to say something mournful. The men laughed at him. Maldonado rolled in his hammock and said, "Rather high strung for country people, wouldn't you say, Louis? And they so despise your climsiness." Louis, kicking futilely at the cat, returned to his room.

Katy decided to do the same and met Art on his way out. "Don't," she said. "We don't want to go out there for a while yet."

Stubbornly ignorant of each other and lacking any will to wound, the Barnetts could not afford frequent disagreement. Their few quarrels had sustained themselves, tepidly, forever.

"Maybe we could have stayed here; it might have been kind of nice. But now I think we'd better not."

"Why?"

"Because I don't want to."

"But I do," Art said.

"Then why did you have to go and tell that arrogant old fart everything there is to know about us? Did you tell him about Aunt Leota's hen? That's how interesting we are, Art. We're like something that lays an egg every day."

"What?"

"You don't know the first thing about him," she said. "And now you tell me he's come up with some kind of plan."

"For one thing I know he's not really arrogant. That's just his style. You have to admit, he does have style."

"I'll admit I never should have sent you down to breakfast alone. Did he tell you what he's doing here?"

"Doing? He's got to be retired by now. He's way older than we are, Katy."

"He's not quite retired yet," she said. "He's up to something."

"Sure. I mean, how much could he be up to . . . here?"

"You tell me, Art. Didn't you just say you wanted to . . . Did you ask him how he made his money?"

"That would be kind of impolite, wouldn't it? Katy, you're going to like him when you get to know him better--To tell you the truth, I don't care whether you like him or not. I don't get a chance to meet people like this every day and I . . ."

"People like what?"

"Put it this way, he's not the kind of guy you bump into in the faculty lounge, and he's not the kind of guy who has to worry whether or not some kid's going to sideswipe his car in the parking lot."

"How do you know what he does or doesn't worry about?"

"You lied about those desks," Art said. "That's not even my job. It's Mr. Erickson's. And we do it in June. You knew that."

"What am I supposed to do if we stay?" said Katy, changing tack, losing patience. "What am I supposed to think when you won't even tell me what you've got going on?"

"I don't see why you have to be doing something every minute. This is a vacation. The whole idea is to relax. Here we finally get to a place I like--" His eyes searched the ceiling in an excess of innocence that always disarmed her. Did he, could he affect this purposely? It was not like him to want anything this much. "It's peaceful here," he finally said.

An arhythmic sounding at the doorframe. Just Louis' head, breaching, beaming in. His breath filled the room with the smell of juniper berries. "Ready, Katy?"

"I've just been telling Art that I'm not sure I feel like it."

"You'd miss our mission to the mission?"

"I imagine you've seen it a thousand times," Katy said.

"Just twice. It's fabulous."

"It's really supposed to be," Art said.

"Why aren't you coming, then?" she asked her husband. "If this is such a vital attraction, what's holding you back?"

"I told you, I want to talk over some business with Sean."

"Yeah, and then you told me that he wasn't in business. You said that about two minutes ago. Remember?"

"It's too indefinite right now. I didn't want to say anything and get your hopes up."

"Get my hopes up? That's the last thing you have to worry about. You tell the man that he can forget it. Whatever it is he's got in mind, he can forget it."

"We'll make it a fun day," Louis assured her. "We'll have a lot more fun than they do because we're the kind of people who know how to have fun."

Through no fault of his own, Louis had become tolerable to her. If not trustworthy. "Louis," she said, "you can't talk and drive at the same . . . hey! You shouldn't be swerving on this road." Along the river a one-room hut housed three generations of a fisherman's family not far from the place on the bank where the fisherman, with consummate stupidity, cleaned his daily catch. Katy avoided looking at these people.

Accustomed now to Louis, she looked at him. They went first to the ice cream parlor, Katy's treat, and Louis explained that dátil was date, a flavor one could safely dismiss. "But the vanilla is almost perfect, wouldn't you say? Katy? Remember now, we're splurging, we're having fun."

"Wonderful," she said. "The vanilla is. I was . . . I guess I was just having a little attack of homesickness."

"To me," Louis said, "that's the most romantic of all--homesickness."

"Really?"

"It must be a very pure form of despair."

"I wouldn't go that far," Katy said. "Not yet. You know what I keep thinking about? Every fall the wind piles our birch and maple leaves against the Orange Street side of our fence. It catches them there and makes a kind of a wild sound. It sounds like somebody's trying to tell you something. That's what keeps popping up in my head. It'll be happening pretty soon after we get home."

"Leaves?" Louis said.

"The sound."

"Hm. Did you know there's a long distance terminal in the market across the street? If you want to call the States, they can put one through for you. But they nick you for it; damn phone people charge you like they're trying to clear up the national debt."

Because the charges were reversible, Katy thought she could afford to call her son. She spoke to him from a phone nailed to a post between bins of chilis and onion. "Carl? Can you hear me?" Of course he could hear her. He'd never had a bad connection in his life, didn't know they were possible. He wanted to know how things were. Like an oven, she told him. As long as it was different, he said. Had they seen whales mate? Had they bought him a serape? In the background a girl's voice asked after baking powder.

"It looks like we'll be getting back a day or two later than we said we would," Katy told her son. "Your dad wants to stay over a while."

"Dad wants to?"

"For a day or two," she said. Her voice was calm, false.

"I'll be in Evanston by the time you get back. Mrs. Strickland said she'd come over and feed Ace."

"Carl--did I hear you call that girl Paula? That wouldn't be Mrs. Perry's Paula?"

"Mom, she's just . . ."

"Oh no--I'm not saying anything. I trust you two. But . . . she is young."

"Hello?" he said. "Mom?"

"I trust your judgment, Carl, but I'm not so sure about your taste. Be good, Honey."

"Mom?" he said again.

Katy rejoined Louis at a pharmacy where the pharmacist abandoned a joke in mid-sentence as she came through the door. Chin tucked into the collar of his smock, the man seemed unwilling to let her see the right side of his face. "We'll be going on foot from here," said Louis. "Thought I'd better get something to numb the old stub. I hope you're feeling adventurous, Katy. I know I am." He was on the verge of reeling.

They went further upriver, crossed a weir. The biggest sow Katy had ever seen lay tethered to a tree. Twists of interesting undergrowth gave way within a quarter mile to an abused fringe of upland pasture. Beyond that the path gained quickly to a palisade overlooking the river. Though well placed, the mission was disappointing at first as an expression of faith. They walked the building's perimeter. Katy had expected that it would at least be whitewashed. "The padres built these things on high ground," Louis said. "The Indians they were trying to convert ate the seeds from their own excrement. Treacherous clientele." Katy saw the chapel, a structure of stone hand hewn to right angles, as a monument to terrible effort. "This thing was here through the Empire," Louis told her. "And all through the Revolution. It'll be here when there's nothing left but ants."

"Ants?"

"After Armageddon," Louis said.

"Oh. I thought that big building was the mission. The one you can see from down in Proviso. It's got that cross on it."

"That was the state prison. Baja Sur."

"With the hawks flying around?"

"Buzzards," Louis corrected. "You can tell by the red around their necks. That's where it's fleshy, so they don't mat their feathers when they dip into carrion."

"Big prison, little church. Kind of fits, doesn't it."

"Fits? How do you mean?"

"I'm not sure," Katy said.

Louis dully appraised the emptiness north of them. "It wasn't a bad prison, as prisons go. The inmates were released every morning. Then at night, around five, a bell was rung and they'd go back to dinner. They were only under lock and key at night. The cells were somewhat barbaric, but . . . Quite a few of the men had their families in town. Some of them even ran businesses."

"They didn't want to escape?"

"I'm sure they did, but where would they go?" The story of the prisoner's benign confinement settled Louis; he spoke of it with respect and even longing. "Until a few years ago, you couldn't get to Santa Rosalia in less than a day. By jeep. A man couldn't carry enough water to walk that far. So they had a choice; they could sleep in prison or come out here and try their luck with the desert and the Federales. The place had a spotless record."

"Yeah," said Katy, "I think I know that scheme."

"You've lost me again," Louis told her.

The timbers of the church door had long since twisted its iron hinges, and a dust like corn starch had blown in. But it was, Katy thought, a place of astonishing cleanliness. A single vaulted chamber lit by votive candles and the few narrow slits cut high in its walls. Behind the altar, a plaster Christ, his anatomy sculpted improbably, his wounds extensive. There were crepe paper flowers and rows of wooden benches worn smooth. So little light, but all of it so pure. Katy discovered herself pressing the flat of her hand to her heart.

"I've got a commission," Louis said.

"Isn't it spooky in here? In kind of a nice way. Nice and cool."

"I've got a commission," Louis repeated happily. "From Sean. I'm going to paint you."

"Paint me? Why in the world would you want to paint me?"

"Because El Jefe's paying me a hundred and fifty dollars to do it. Or the equivalent in pesos. Don't get me wrong, now. It's not as if there wouldn't be artistic satisfaction in it. You'll make a fascinating subject."

This, she understood, had been largely responsible for his mood. "I know what I look like," she said, "and . . . Well, I know what I look like."

"You're in Latin America, Katy, and you're a strawberry blond. In our eyes, that makes you an idol. That's not the word--an ideal."

They went outside where the day had continued brilliant. Despite herself, Katy was flattered. White woman, indisputably that. Thinking about it confused her. The celebrated pallor of Katy Barnett. Pasty Face, as she had once been styled.

Louis smiled at her.

Trying to disguise whatever it was she was feeling as girlishness, Katy climbed the hand and foot holds cut into an escarpment behind the church. She sat carefully on a ledge commanding the whole progress of the river. Louis climbed up after her. Winded and in pain, he said, "This is dangerous."

"If you think it's dangerous, get down."

Louis clung to the rock, looking, eventually, thoughtful. He nodded toward Proviso. "I don't know how they live in that. Cocks crowing all night, damned dogs barking."

"Who were those men your boss was talking to this morning?"

"I don't have a boss."

"Who are they? Are you afraid of them?"

"I'm afraid of almost everyone," Louis said. "It's been my experience that people aren't naturally kind to me. And that's so unfair because . . ."

"Why do you suppose he wants a picture of me?"

"The working artist has to make a real point of not second guessing any form of patronage, Katy. No matter what tastelessness is required of you. And here we have opportunity without compromise. Who cares what he wants with it, we're going to really . . . you and I, we'll . . ."

"How does he make his money?"

"Sean? He hasn't got any serious money."

"But he's got some."

"Everyone has a little," Louis said. "Even I will now. You know what I wish we had? A camel's hair coat. I was thinking I'd need to order some new brushes . . . That complexion against the texture of camel's hair. Can you imagine it?"

Far below them the river carried an empty dory around a long bend and on down to the sea.

Canvases lay two deep on easels, stacked against the walls, broken at the foot of his bed. Louis most wanted her to see those with snapshots still stapled to their corners. "Keep in mind," he said again, "that my style isn't strictly representational. I'm far more concerned with finding an essence than reproducing a mere likeness." Katy put her hand to her mouth in a way she hoped would look deliberative. His subjects were: the desert, its shapes pointlessly softened; a broad mauve smear, inspired, he claimed, by Mrs. Yee's back; the rocker in the courtyard; a number of bovinely posed tourists. His work was not as crude as finger painting.

"They're better than I could do," Art said.

Maldonado held a still life of a bowl and an apple at arm's length, tilted his head for perspective. "I hope you won't disgrace yourself like this with my piece, Louis. Most of these things look like they were done at a therapy session."

"Of course they do," Louis said impatiently. "Tools. That's exactly what I've been trying to tell you." He offered a glass filled with brushes and gum spirits as evidence. "With mops like these, about all you can hope for is . . ."

"Give yourself every advantage," Maldonado told him, pointedly relieved to be leaving the room. "You'll have to find a way to improve on this. I had forgotten how . . . You will give this your best effort?"

They moved as a group across the courtyard, out to the tip of the promontory. Katy stood with Louis, heat radiating up through planking and sandal, and watched her proudly laden husband descend a long wooden stair to a boathouse. He carried down tanks, a mask, a pick and shovel.

"You'd think," Katy said, "that with all that gear they would have managed to come back with something. Fish, a seashell. Something."

"Oh, the fish are thick out there," Louis told her. "A length of line, a fish hook, and nothing but a bottle cap for bait--you could feed a whole family out of these waters with just that. I'm sure they've been catching something. Sean throws them back in. It's sport with him."

Maldonado's boat nosed from the boathouse. Mahogany hull, she'd been told. Art turned as the launch gunned toward open water. He started to wave back at them, thought better of it, folded his arms, and faced forward again. Feet spread wide, master of his destiny.

"We'd better get started," Katy said.

"The light is very bad now," Louis said. "It couldn't be much worse."

"If you want that fee, you'd better plan on making

hay while the sun shines. I'm going to try to get us out of here as early as possible tomorrow."

"Farmers are concerned with hay," Louis said. "To my everlasting gratitude, I am not a farmer."

"You can't paint me if I'm not here."

"I'd like someone, just once, to appreciate that there are a few requirements for creativity. I need time, I need equipment. Disgrace myself--the man's tastes are decidedly pedestrian."

"But my point is," Katy said gently, "that you won't have much time to get this done."

"Oh? Your plans may not . . ."

"May not what?"

"You're right," Louis said. "We'll find some shade. We'll make the best of a bad situation. I didn't live in the States all those years without learning something. The old American get up and go. Have you tried Bacardi and 7-Up? Makes a fine early morning drink. With the right inspiration, I can sometimes work very quickly, very instinctively."

Half an hour later Louis was studying her with an almost creditable air of fascination. From time to time he sneered at his sketch pad as if it were purposely thwarting him. He held a chunk of charcoal like a short black baton but resisted any impulse to put it to paper. His instincts were on holiday. Katy posed in the sun. "You know how the Moslems won't have their pictures taken?" she said. "It's the Moslems or somebody. They think it captures their souls. That's me. Not the part about the souls, but . . . I don't know. We used to go down to the photographer's studio on the first business day after Thanksgiving and have our picture taken. I hated that, hated that worse than anything I can remember."

"I'm intrigued that you mention souls," Louis said. "When I reach the height of my powers, I'll be capturing souls. In my art. Don't move." He slashed decisively at the sketch pad. "Now, remember, this is just the basis for what we're going to do later. But I think this little piece, just as it is, has about as much integrity as anything I've ever done." He turned the pad toward her. She was represented there by three thick streaks, a slantwise triangle. "Try to be open minded."

"I like it," she said. "That's good, Louis. You've really caught me. That's quite something."

"You've missed it completely," he said. "This is pure emotion."

"No. I mean it."

"In that case, it's yours. For--two hundred dollars."

"Mr. Big pays only a hundred and fifty. And that's for one with color and everything."

"Sean is a buyer's market."

Kathy thought she recognized an opening. "Who is he?"

"What do you mean?"

"You know what I mean. Where's he from, originally?"

"He's a Chicano," Louis said with distaste. "And I only know that because he lapses into their grimy little patois sometimes."

"But you've know him for--for years, I take it."

"He's got the good sense not to bore me with the details of his past."

"Look, my husband is not a very worldly man, and he's gotten himself involved with . . . I'm afraid he might be in over his head. All this mystery is a little frightening. Art's never held anything from me. I'll be so happy to get out of here.''

''Why do you keep talking about leaving us, Katy? You can't imagine how much I've enjoyed your company.''

''Why would I stay? No offense, but--why? It's been two days already, and that's two days more than we meant to stay. There's really nothing for me to do here.''

''I would think you could stay long enough to be immortalized,'' Louis said. ''And--Spanish lessons. I was a guest lecturer one semester at the University of Guadalajara. You wouldn't believe how fast you'll pick it up with professional instruction.''

''Why won't they tell me what they're doing, Louis?''

''Why would you even be curious? I know Sean, and I think I've come to know Art pretty well, and I'm sure whatever they're doing wouldn't interest either one of us in the least. We're cut from different cloth, Katy. No matter what happens, we'll have at least that much to be thankful for.''

Dinner was served that evening in a room large enough to have once contained dancing, its ceiling so tall as to suspend cobwebs above the reach of Mrs. Yee's broom. Small sets of sharks' jaws, still poised to tear, were ranked on the walls around them. Smoke from Maldonado's cigar rose in fluid layers like magician's scarves. He lived, Katy had noticed, almost entirely on these cigars. She concentrated to avoid nausea.

''You're not also suffering the *cruda*, Mrs. Barnett?''

''You're unusually pale. Were you drinking with Louis?''

"No."

"I hope that foot isn't acting up on him," Art said.

"Could you put that thing out, Mr. Maldonado?" Katy asked her host. "It's a bit much in a confined space like this."

"Do you know what I exchange for these?" Maldonado asked her. "Gold. I leave a small ingot on deposit at a bank in Tampa. I know the name of the man who rolls my cigars. I know his wife's name. You'll find this smoke ambrosial when you've accustomed yourself to it."

Katy's head hovered above a dulled, diminished body, a momentary effect of the acrid air. She tried to sustain the sensation.

"As for Louis," Maldonado told her husband, "he's a hypochondriac and may well die some day from a completely imaginary ailment."

"If he's sick," Katy said, "he's sick."

"Not in any way worthy of your sympathy. Do you know what happened to his foot?"

"He never talks about it," Art said.

"I wouldn't either. It's an ingrown toenail."

"The poor man must be in agony," Katy said. "That can be quite serious."

"It certainly is in his case. He can't stand to let anyone touch it, so it has never been treated properly. He can't stand needles, either, and won't believe antibiotics can be given in any other way. The man's capacity for foolishness is just about unlimited. Risking infection."

Katy felt a clot, a bubble moving up through her. It surfaced as a giggle. She saw this alert something in Maldonado. He talked of home remedies, the ministrations of many quacks. The topic disgusted him in a way he seemed to relish. ". . . up well past the ankle. Green. Louis was terrified, as he usually is, quite certain that someone would be coming around any day to insist that it be cut off. The herbalist was finally able to convince him that they'd only dyed his foot. So much for the ocotillo poultice. Louis actually let the charlatan administer another. It smelled like--roofing tar."

It came again, unexpected and unwelcome. Katy could not have said why, but she knew that she was going to laugh. Something bad and buoyant. Jets of consommé shot from her nostrils.

He groaned, twitched, groaned again, louder. "Under the eaves," he said, then snorted. Art lay beside her, silent and still, for a long time. She had told him earlier that she would leave tomorrow, with or without him, that she was never again going to breathe anything of Maldonado's. And he had told her that she was welcome to leave if she thought she had to. She felt him wake up.

"Katy?"

She said nothing.

"Katy?"

Once, early in their marriage, Katy had suffered a month of influenza. Her convalescence would become, perversely, a memory, an emotional token she had rung up at least once a week ever since. Art solicitous. He had revealed himself as an instinctively kind man. He had read to her from *Heidi*, his still young voice realizing all the joy in phrases like "I'd rather go like the goats, with their swift little legs." A sweet man who'd never understood what was best in him as anything but a social liability.

How many times had they spoken each other's names? The familiar voice. "Katy," he said, and she knew that he was afraid. They were linked still by a conduit of shared sensitivity. Strangers living in each other's guts.

Katy knocked at the door of Louis' room.

"Yes?"

"Louis, it's me." From inside came another response, muffled, impatient. Katy let herself in. "Louis?" His bloated face rose, somewhat alarmed, above the back of an armchair. A heroic welt had been inscribed down one cheek by an upholsterer's seam. He blinked furiously. "Shut the door."

"Have you recovered from yesterday?" she asked him. "You look awful."

"I know," he said. "I keep forgetting to move." He held up for her approval a broken volume. "Jane Austen. Every year I read her complete works, more or less in one sitting. It's hell on me. Art told us this morning at breakfast that you'll be leaving today. I'll miss you."

Katy sat on the arm of his chair, took his wrist, squeezed it lightly. "If you know anything about what those two are up to, you have to tell me. You have to, Louis."

"Sean cancelled on the painting, anyway. He gets so impatient when his demands aren't met instantly."

Katy took a tighter grip, and, inadvertently, Louis' pulse.

"Sometimes," he said, "I'll finish *Pride and Prejudice* and go right on to the Brontës."

"Louis."

"Look, if you don't know what they're doing, how would I? Ask your husband. Ask Sean. They know. I don't."

"I've been asking them. I'm not getting anywhere." She was a little surprised at the ease of this lie. Not since that first day had she asked her husband about the nature of his dealings. She had never asked Maldonado. She understood that she kept asking Louis because he might not know, and if he did, he would never tell. She was asking Louis because she really didn't want to know.

"You must have noticed." Louis said, "that my complete disinterest in Sean's doings is my stock in trade. What is that you're wearing?" She had fashioned a sort of burnoose from a sheet. She told him that she was going walking and needed protection from the sun. "Clever," he said. "So--does this mean you're not leaving?"

"I guess I can't," she said.

She spent her mornings in the desert, equipped with a canteen of coppery tasting water. Every blade of grass a palpable miracle, every stunted shrub and blinking lizard a self-sufficient wonder. Ferrous streaks of red worked large patterns in the odorless earth. The companionable territory of the morning.

But in the afternoons, when the heat was not to be attempted, Katy stayed in the room. Alone and without duties, she was invisible to herself. What she had understood as her personality was no more than a series of obligations, no more than habit, and now, having set most of that aside, there was very little left.

Waxy sheets of Correo par Avion stationery papered a swath of floor around the dresser.

Dear Susan,

They sure weren't kidding about the slow pace of life down here. Thought I'd use the time to drop you a line. That rhymed. We've been

Dear Susan,

Not exactly having a great time but I wish you were here anyway. About the only news from here is that Art has a real sun tan. The man we're staying with has a boat and they go out in it every day. Art has learned to scuba dive. At least he tells me he has. I must say he looks pretty healthy.

I've been rubbing myself with aloe vera cuttings. Doesn't prevent me from peeling. I've shed as much skin as a garter snake.

Don't know why I'm writing this. I'll bet I'm sitting in your kitchen on the day it gets delivered.

Dear Susan,

If something should come up so that we can't get back by August 17th, would you call Mr. Woodrell and tell him that we'll

Dear Susan,

Dear, dear Susan

Through the small window in the door she could see that part of the courtyard where Art and Maldonado passed the latter part of the day together, and it was with brutal fascination that she watched her husband's nodding head, obsessive agreement working it almost like palsy.

Mrs. Yee came in the early evenings with a dinner tray. Mrs. Yee, frail and unapproachable as a sparrow.

Katy imagined that the old woman must hold a hard opinion of the gringa who, in her petulant arrogance, refused to eat with the men.

And every night, when Art climbed the stairs, the Barnetts would, by tacit but invariable arrangement, go immediately to bed. Katy no longer spoke to him of home or of anything else. They lay back to back. The cadences of his breathing told her that he slept less than three hours a night. Everything had been said.

Mardo Avellano surely would have broken into a run if his arms had been free. He grunted down the dock toward them, carrying a picnic basket as big as a bassinet, Miguelito right at his heels, yipping, "Ay, ay, ayyy," in celebration of his authority over the newest member of Maldonado's little staff.

"Remember to look back when we get about a quarter mile out," Art told her. "Punta Coyote, it's called. Supposed to look like a coyote's snout. Personally, I can't see it."

It was seven o'clock in the morning. Mrs. Yee came down the stairs, bent under a bale of blankets.

"Did you recognize that big kid?" Katy asked. "He was on the bus."

"Him and eight hundred others."

"You talked to his family."

"I didn't talk to that kid. I don't think there'd be much point in trying to . . ." Reflexively, Art turned away from her. "I can hardly wait for you to see this."

"Too late," she said. "Comes too late. You didn't want to let me in on it--all right. I lost interest. I don't even want to learn the secret handshake."

"That's it. That's the attitude right there. Why we've been keeping you in the dark. You have to be an optimist to make good things happen."

Maldonado came, preceded by his cigar and followed by Louis who took the stairs with boundless caution, one at a time, making as much as possible of his foot. Descent required a technique he did not seem to know.

Maldonado was tired, he had said, of so unsociable an atmosphere. He boarded them all. A composition in pillows and sticks, Mrs. Yee manned the aft seat cushion, her tiny cone of chin propped high by a life jacket. Art, Katy, Louis, Miguelito, and Mardo Avellano were arranged in a horseshoe around her, intent, Katy thought, as a pickup load of dogs, oppressed by the raging engine, lost in themselves. The boat pounded across the grain of a lightly rolling sea. The man at the wheel, Katy recalled, had said that all places could be mean. He kept them within hailing distance of a rough shore, headed north.

Finally they came to an interruption in the tedium of the coast, a half mile crescent of white sand containing a jewel of a lagoon. Maldonado throttled back. Katy made out footprints on the beach, meaningfully placed cairns. The engine stopped. Though the inlet enjoyed good protection from the surf, Maldonado dropped anchor in fifteen feet of water. "We can't get out here," Katy said. "Why don't you go in a little closer so we can all get out? If I'm going to look at this, I'd like to . . ."

"We're going to be diving first," Maldonado explained. "At this depth the boat makes an excellent diving platform."

"Great. In the meantime the rest of us are sitting up here getting burned to a crisp."

"There are parasols for everyone, Mrs. Barnett. And for you, a mask and fins. Please pay attention, this may be the best day of your life.''

Youthfully, expertly, Art and Maldonado shrugged into their diving gear. Art found no apparent satisfaction in his new skill. He was more muscular and lean than he'd been in years. And distracted. Maldonado rolled overboard backward. Louis and the others sat in the shade of their parasols, already bored to stone.

''Spit into your mask,'' Art told her. ''That's right, spit. Now rub it around on the glass. Keeps it from fogging up.'' He showed her how to hold the snorkle tube in her mouth, helped her lower herself over the side, taught her to trust her face to the water. ''Then you just breathe and kick,'' he said. ''Relax. Breathe, kick. That's good. That's . . . You've got it.'' She heard him swim away from her.

Breathe, kick. It was just that easy. She had learned effortless motion. Green bars of light swayed on the sand below her. At the least volition she slid along, one with the glinting fish. Bright fish in a warm saline medium; and fun. There was nothing, she thought, much stranger to her than fun. And here . . . here . . . She soared the whole length of the lagoon. Katy swam until she was tired, and would have kept swimming but for a school of needle-nosed fish. They swarmed around her. When they began to glance off her thighs, she panicked. Suddenly there was saltwater in her snorkel. She thrashed toward the boat.

Louis reached down to receive her flippers as she came alongside. ''Jelly fish?''

''I don't know what they were,'' she said. ''We'd call them gar. The kind of fish people shoot with .22's back home. But this is exhilarating. It'll be a few minutes before I can, you know, breathe naturally again, but I'm going to . . . Did you want to . . . Have you seen the other two?''

Louis' arm swept the horizon to indicate that they were somewhere under the world's water and that it didn't matter where. He helped her into the boat.

''Do you know how long they can stay down,'' she asked him.

''Forever, as far as I'm concerned.''

Wild at the wheel, Miguelito bounced on the captain's chair, his lips aflutter in a fair imitation of an inboard motor. The rest of the crew sat entirely mute for what seemed to Katy a surreal amount of time, Mardo to port, Mrs. Yee to starboard, staring fixedly through each other.

''If you're not feeling up to this,'' Katy said, ''you shouldn't let them drag you out here, Louis.''

''Another indignity,'' he agreed. ''I'm addicted to misery.''

''You should try a change of scene.''

''Oh, absolutely. I was thinking about touring the Continent. The Rothschilds keep sending me tickets.''

''You could get out of here,'' Katy said, ''if you really wanted to.''

''You have the means to leave,'' Louis said flatly. ''And--here you are.''

''We're leaving. We're leaving tomorrow.''

''We? Both of you?''

''We have to,'' she said. ''I see on the map that there's an airport in Guaymas. If we catch the ferry over tomorrow morning, and we can get a flight out to Texas or Arizona, I think we can make it back in time for our first classes.''

''And Art is going with you?''

''Didn't I just say . . . We have to go. We have to get

back to work.''

Louis avoided her eyes. ''I've made so many mistakes. But this . . .'' He looked off toward the shallows where Art and Maldonado's fins flicked like the noses of feeding trout at the surface of the water.

Katy felt the chill of his sympathy and folded her parasol. ''They're letting me in on the big secret today. Art's at the point where he can hardly hold it in. Two grown men . . . I can't believe it; it's like they joined a boys' club.''

''A boys' club,'' Louis said. ''Not exactly. I imagine it's more dismal than that.''

''You're really in pain.''

''Perpetually,'' he said.

''Isn't there a doctor in Santa Rosalia?''

''There's a doctor in Proviso,'' he said. ''Doctors are like houseflies; they're everywhere. Katy, the idiot is staring at you.''

''He's harmless.''

''*Basta, tonto. Basta.*''

''Quit it, Louis. Please. You're scaring him.''

As if summoned, Mardo stood, crossed to her, and held a sodden rope of her hair devotedly in his hands.

''*Basta. Basta. Suéltala.*''

''Please, Louis. Please be quiet. He's only curious.''

Maldonado surfaced thirty feet astern and swam steadily to the boat. He climbed in, trembling, water sluicing through the hairy cleft of his chest. On the deck lay a long fiberglass rod Katy had assumed to be a simple speargun, at one end, a loop of surgical tubing, at the other, three long steel tines. When Maldonado picked it up, she knew he meant to kill with it. Art came up at the back of the lagoon. Maldonado pulled a rubber boot from the end of the tines and they sprung free of each other, vibrating. He brought the pole around in a long graceful arc, like a golf swing, and the tines tore the upper slope of Mardo Avellano's back. Mardo gasped, threw himself at Mrs. Yee's feet. Katy heard Louis whimper. She picked up an air tank from the engine housing, the cylinder as light as an idea in her hands. Katy raised the cylinder above her head and brought it down. She beat at the gunwale again and again until flakes of ancient shellac blew away like flint.

"It was disrespect for his guests. He had to. You don't understand their code."

"You don't beat retarded people, Art. You just don't do that."

"He only hit him once."

"Art, start packing." She slid a drawer from the dresser and emptied its contents with a flourish onto the bed. "I don't know how I let it get this far out of hand. I knew something was wrong with him. Now, what was going on. All of it."

"That's what I wanted to show you. All that work, all that planning. I don't see why we have to . . ." Art settled carefully onto a hassock and sat there, his hands limp in his lap. "We could have had this place," he said.

He briefly related a deal that called for him to build Maldonado a new house at the lagoon. Art was to receive the Excelsior as compensation.

"What good would that do us?" she asked him. "Who was supposed to run it for us?"

"We were going to run it. We still could."

"No," she said. "No. No. This mausoleum? You have to be out of your mind."

"I need to talk to him, Katy."

"No you don't. I'm not going to live here," she said. "That's all you need to know. There is no deal. We're leaving. We're not even going to ask them for a ride back into town."

"You were the one who wanted something new," Art said resolutely. "I have to talk to him."

She watched him through the window, crossing the courtyard. His thongs caused him to walk in a deliberate, disjointed way that somehow saddened her. He entered Maldonado's apartment without knocking. Katy followed him.

Maldonado's room was of the same size and configuration as Louis', but had a window facing onto the courtyard. At this hour light slanted against the glass, nearly rendering it opaque. Katy came quite close. Inside, Maldonado stood a foot in front of Art, looking up at him. His voice was low but precise. She heard the more emphatic words. "Now . . ." Maldonado was saying. ". . . not in one lifetime . . . Never again." Art backed a step away from him, wincing. Why couldn't the old man stop humiliating everyone? The room was segmented by long tables loaded with potted hyacinths. There was a sleeping pallet with some books scattered around it, a reading light, an alarm clock. The furnishings of an especially poor college student. The association touched her. Idiotic. "Limits," she heard Maldonado say. And again, ". . . limits."

Then Sean Maldonado reached up to take her husband's head in his hands. He held it as if it were a child's head--firm and gentle, his thumbs hooked into the cranial bones behind Art's ears. Katy could hear nothing of what he was saying now, but she could see that it was meant to soothe. Maldonado slowly drew his fingertips across Art's cheeks, pressed them to her husband's lips.

Katy rapped on the window.

They turned toward her. Art blanched. His mouth formed the word: "I."

They had contained themselves for some many years. Katy would have postponed this business of weeping for another twenty years if she'd had a choice. She told herself that she'd chosen none of this. Art whimpered like a child. A child, she thought, and he'd have had his cheeks slapped rosy. The Ford nudged through a crowded backstreet, Santa Rosalía's laundry district. It was as clean as a church-sponsored carnival.

"We might as well get out and look around," she said.

The town had more than its share of happy children. A singing barber, a flower vendor's creaking purple cart. Everywhere, the evidence of Santa Rosalía's luck and pleasure in itself. A crowd of women yelled like open air commodities brokers at a crew of bakers filling glass cases with thousands of flour powdered biscuits. Katy bought a sweet roll and continued down the street. Art trailed her, his eyes swollen, brimming again. She led him into an entirely metal church. A placard in the apse said in English, Spanish, and French that this church had been originally constructed in Paris by none other than Monsieur Eiffel, then taken down in pieces and shipped, along with sheaves of schematic drawing, to the wrong Santa Rosalía. It had been meant for the Jesuits in Chile. Lucky town.

Art wiped his nose with the back of his hand. "Can I leave now?" he asked her. "There's no point in me hanging around."

"What a religious country this is," she said.

"Katy, this is torture. Dragging it out is only going to make it worse."

"I'm going to have lunch," she said. "Then you're going to drive me to the pier. Do you have any of your traveler's checks left? Give them to me."

Just outside the church a boy with boxes slung from his shoulders fell into step behind them and chattered and mocked until Katy bought his tamales and a bottle of beer. The boy stood banging his dirty knees together. He watched with satisfaction as she ate. Sweat beaded her upper lip. "You'd better have something," she told her husband. "You'll need your strength tonight."

"You don't have to try and make me feel bad," Art said, "I feel bad already."

"Oh, you do? I'm sorry to hear that. Tell me something, what happens to Louis now?"

"He . . . ? Oh. Nothing. He's . . ."

"Straight?"

"Yeah."

"Don't be too sure about that. That's the kind of thing you just can't take for granted these days." The boy who'd sold her the tamales had crossed the street and was pointing them out to one of his friends.

"I told you, Katy, I'm not that way, either."

"Oh, but you are. You couldn't do it with him if you didn't like it."

"I did it because I wanted . . ."

"Shut up," she said. Calm suffused her.

Though it was dangerously hot, they waited in the car for the ferry to berth. The pilot made three ponderous stabs at her mooring. "I'm going to get my ticket,"

Katy said. "You'd better be here when I come out of that building."

"You know I wouldn't just leave you. And--you don't have to go. I don't want you to go."

"Wait for me," she said.

The report of her wooden-heeled shoes against the floor filled the big administration building. Katy pushed bills of meaningless denominations under a brass grille, and the clerk pushed back two tickets. "Buen viaje," he said.

Outside, Art waited for her at the top of the pedestrian passengers' loading ramp. When she approached him, he leaned down to finger the handle of her suitcase. Then he stood up again. "I don't know what to say," he told her.

"Don't say anything. Just get on the boat."

"Katy, I thought we'd decided . . . I'm sorry."

"You already said that."

"The only thing I know for sure is that I can't go back. Not now. You were right. What we had at home wasn't enough. I know that now. I really am sorry."

"You only think you're sorry, Mister. You're getting on this boat. Right now. Or everything you had is mine. How hard do you think it would be for me to arrange that?"

"You think I don't know what I'm giving up? Don't you know I've been thinking about that constantly? But I found out I want to be my own man. I want that hotel. Something that's mine."

"I don't much care what you think you need, Art. Now, here's the deal: you're getting on this boat because if you don't, the first thing I do when I get back home is go over and have a chat with your mother."

"You said you'd had enough of me. You said you

couldn't forgive me."

"What happens to dear old Mavis' Puritan heart when I tell her that her son is a fairy? And I'd have to tell her."

"I'm not . . ."

"Mavis, Carl, the Lions' Club. I won't cover for you, Art. I'd make sure everybody knew. You won't get a second chance." Katy walked down the ramp. Art hesitated, hefted the suitcase, and followed her. She gave the purser both tickets.

The Barnetts climbed to the upper deck to lean against the railing. Trucks and cars came rolling on below them. The cargo master denied passage to a farmer and his three cows. It would be a quiet crossing. Crew secured the cargo gate.

"We can't go back to the way things were," Art said. "But I love you, Katy. That never changed."

Propellors were engaged, diesels pulled down into a lower register, men poled from the dock, a tug labored alongside. *La Esperanza* was underway.

"Louis' car," Art remembered.

"They'll find it," Katy said. The shore receded.

"This may surprise you," he said, "but, in a way, I'm kind of honored . . . that you . . . to have someone care enough to . . . All I've got to wear are the clothes on my back. They ought to be ripe by the time we get home. They are already."

They leaned side by side against the railing. And her husband did smell, an odor faint and pleasant in the sea air. Katy noticed that they had assumed exactly the same posture. They stood alike, they spoke alike, and they had shared the same assumptions. Though it might have been useful, she could not think of him as wrong.

"No," she said. "I'm the one who should be sorry. You know what, Art? I don't love you. I've wanted to. I know I'm supposed to. But I don't."

His hands trembled on the railing.

"I could have left you here," she told him. "But it would have been too convenient. It would have been a little too mean. Here I was the one wanting to shake things up, make just anything new happen, and . . . You can change everything that you thought made you what you were, and in the end you haven't changed a thing. I'm going to give you what I always gave you, Art. That and a little piece of advice: We are what we are."

She watched the land behind them flatten to the thickness of paper and slide completely out of sight.

TACOMA

The rooming house where Leonard Diehl was born had been replaced by a cinder-block building with no windows and no apparent purpose. He stood just behind a curtain of sliding gray beads, rain dripping from the awning of the Peerless Luncheonette, and he remembered a Victor Avenue of chipped white paint and flower boxes, the smell of soap being made from lard. Leonard folded a trenchcoat into the crook of his arm and watched himself walk up and down the street. Newly fitted in long pants, he carried a growler of beer home to his father and a gaggle of freeloading uncles; an older child, a walking hard-on, humiliated himself haggling with a frowzy Armenian whore; the sailor home on leave swaggered once more into the lobby of the now absent Empire Theater, a stain blossoming rose-like beneath the USS Roanoke patch where a stevedore's shiv had nicked. Sure. A rosy glow on the whole damn neighborhood. The old life looks good because you were young in it.

Leonard, at fifty-seven, was a small, squarely made man wearing a summer suit, a suntan, a pair of wing tips soaked to the laces. That, he reminded himself, had always been the essence of Victor Avenue. That obstinate chill in your feet. He went into the luncheonette. Steam misted stainless steel behind a vacant counter. A waitress pushed through the swinging door from the kitchen and told him, "You better sit at this end of the counter. There's a draft down there." Nearly fat, nearly pretty, she approached him as if she had been sentenced to do so. "Slow today," she said. "I get really lazy when it's slow like this."

"I can't believe what passes for summer here," he said.

The waitress tore two sheets from a roll of paper towels and suggested he dry his hair. Leonard ordered a cup of Sanka. He waited with a cigarette, the column of ash burning toward his fingers. The kid isn't even curious, he thought. The kid isn't a kid.

A week earlier Leonard had received a note from his attorney, saying, "I don't know who sent this. There was no return address. Assume it was meant for you." Paperclipped to the note was a slightly brittle scrap of obituary announcing the death of Karla Diehl. Leonard sat down. Her time had been too brief and his would be too long. An insistent justice. He would never be beyond her reach. Listed among her survivors was a son, Joseph, also of Tacoma. It would have been Joe who'd sent the clipping.

That was Saturday. On Sunday Leonard drove to Del Mar where he lost a hundred and fifteen dollars at the pari-mutuel window. On Monday he called his secretary and cancelled his appointments. Again he went to the track. The vacation extended day by day, a chastened Leonard letting the other fools bet, leaning on the rail, drinking iced tea, breathing the dust the ponies raised each time they rounded for home.

By Friday the sporting life had also staled. He woke that night faced with a test pattern Indian, the cuffs of his trousers pulled up around his knees. To clear his head he stepped out onto the sundeck, into a gentle San Diego evening and he asked himself, What kind of a guy strings this dime store crap all over his own back yard? His Japanese lanterns--fatuous, undulant, still lit at three in the morning. The hours before the paperboy's delivery were predictable. He felt himself turning down that corroded corridor in his imagination through which Karla and the boy, or their vapors, made their endless retreat.

Leonard showered, spent a good deal of time examining himself in the bathroom mirror. Without being particularly hungry, he made himself breakfast. He drove to Lindbergh Field. Within an hour, he was on a flight north, drinking brandy and eating cashew nuts. He ate a second breakfast at SeaTac International. His stomach was in an uproar. He had survived into a too efficient age. What next?

At an airport gift shop Leonard bought the trenchcoat and a tin of aspirin. He wandered into a tiny arcade and invested five quarters in a video game. The machine spoke to him, taunting his ineptitude. Enough of the airport.

A frail old cabbie drove him to town and reported that his first choice of destination, The Elbow Room, had burned. "I believe the Democrats were still in then," the man said. "Long time ago. How about the P&Q?"

"When we hit town, let's just drive around a while, see the sights."

"I get off shift in fifteen minutes," the cabbie said. The skin on his cheekbone was taut and shiny.

Leonard rode as far as the Diamond Cab Company's garage. "There used to be a tailor in this building," he told the driver. "Maybe that was next door. Made my old man's shirts. Had his whole family in there, sewing, and no heat."

"We've got a stove now," the cabbie said. "Things are better that way. But you couldn't get a shirt made anymore for less than a hundred bucks. Hey, I wish you'd change your mind about walking. It's nasty out there, and my relief would be happy to take you anywhere you want to go."

"What's a little rain?" Leonard asked him.

A church bell joined briefly with the clanging against a pierside hull as he got out of the cab; paper torn from shipping crates dissolved to pulp in the gutters. Ships at anchor. He had once believed every rustbucket to leave this port would find some wonderful tragedy, a boarding party, an oriental reef. Leonard found a phone booth, walked past it, then came back. The directory had been torn from its cable. He called information.

"Yes," said the operator. "It's a new listing under this name," and she intoned a familiar number. Leonard dialed it. The phone at the other end rang several times before the receiver was picked up, dropped, picked up again, and a deep, sleep-thickened voice said, "Hello?"

"Hello," he started. "This is Leonard. Leonard Diehl."

"Who?" The voice incredulous or stupid.

"I'm Leonard. Your . . . you know. Leonard Diehl."

No response.

"Is this Joe?"

"Yeah."

"I'm . . ."

"I heard you."

"I'm in town," Leonard said.

"Oh."

Leonard heard himself turn ridiculous. He invented a story about a business trip and the failure of a rental car. The words seemed to move sideways up his throat. ". . . probably water in the gas line or something. So I called the office, and what do they say? They'll send a wrecker. 'Try National,' they tell me. National won't take my goddamn Gold card. So that leaves me . . . So I was wondering, if you're not too busy, maybe you could give me a lift to the airport?"

"Where are you?"

"Victor and . . . Third. Why don't I meet you at the Peerless Luncheonette? That's still open, isn't it?"

"How would I know?"

"I can be there in five, ten minutes. Okay?"

"All right," Joe had said.

There were five filters in his ashtray and a small pile of empty sugar packets on the counter. Leonard had become the waitress' only interest. She eyed him from behind a rack of cereal boxes. He tilted his chin toward his cup and told her, "I've got Sanka dripping out my ears. Is there a phone in here?"

"On the wall between the restrooms."

"Passed it twice," he said, "didn't notice."

"It's a quarter."

He smiled at her indulgently. He knew the cost of things. Leonard left without using the phone.

Outside, the rain had stopped, having left behind a curious organic odor. Another little walk. Because his legs were heavy, Leonard bent at the waist as an athlete might, stretching himself. Might have gotten into something stupid here. This was over a long time ago.

A small orange car came around the corner, slowly up the street, and stopped in front of him. A Toyota. It was Joe. He wore a quilted black cap. His window slid open. "Hope I didn't make you late for your plane."

"No," Leonard said.

A huge man, Joe unfolded from the car. "You'll have to get in on this side. The other door's wired shut." Much of his face was obscured in a sparse web of beard. A fleshy face. But the nose--Karla's on a larger scale. YMCA stencilled across a stretched sweatshirt. Joe. "How'd you wind up in this part of town?" he asked.

"The old stomping grounds," Leonard said. He slid under the steering wheel, into the passenger's seat. "Your mother and I lived here too. When we were first married. Before you were born."

"I knew that. Where's your luggage?"

"Don't have any."

"Not even a briefcase?"

Leonard thought that Joe's suspicion had a glossy, well-used quality about it. "Is there a decent steakhouse around here? My plane doesn't leave until eight."

"You know she's . . ."

"I got the thing you sent."

Joe said that she had been sick a long time, hospitalized for some months, but that her voice had been a foghorn to the end. Leonard had forgotten her voice. She was, he learned, four months gone. The tires skiffed occasionally through standing water.

"I can't afford to eat out," Joe said.

"It's covered. Think I'm cheap or something?"

"No. I've got some hamburger that has to be cooked today."

They continued toward a better part of town along tree-lined thoroughfares. Leonard's first ambition hadn't taken him far. Only ten minutes by car from Victor Avenue, South Florence had once offered space and comparative quiet to those escaping Tacoma's tireder addresses. The neighborhood was so much what it had been during Leonard's time there that the cars in the driveways, the bikes and tricycles, everything of recent origin seemed out of place. They came to the 900 block and a dormered bungalow. In 1955 Leonard had considered the dormers a very classy feature. Ridiculous to a more experienced eye. A lot of trouble to fill an attic with natural light. The glider was missing from the porch.

"Pink? Who painted it pink?"

"Peach," Joe said. "I'm trying to sell the place."

As there was no place to sit in the kitchen, Leonard waited in the living room while Joe cooked. The room had been partially stripped, various pieces of furniture commemorated by dents in the carpet. It was smaller than he remembered. Under Karla's influence the place had been airy, neat. The curtains had been thrown open every morning. Now her flock of porcelain sheep grazed the dusty surfaces of a Hammond organ among empty beer bottles, bills, and a framed graduation picture of Joe that Leonard considered stealing. The kid had been fairly handsome without the beard, more alert looking.

Joe joined him on the couch and set a plate of hamburger smothered in catsup on a footlocker, his table. "I thought you said you were hungry."

They sat in a pile of blankets that gave forth a stale

smell whenever it was disturbed.

"You're living here alone?" Leonard asked.

"I moved back in a few months before Mom went to the hospital. It's been kind of strange. Beats paying rent, though. You thought somebody else lived here?"

"You're still single, then."

"Couldn't be singler."

"That's good," Leonard said.

"It is, huh?"

"What kind of work do you do?"

"Machine shop. Welding mostly."

"You're like your mother. Good with your hands."

"What's that supposed to mean?"

"Nothing. I'm just saying it's best to have a trade. That way you're never out of work."

"I've been laid off the last six months."

"Don't worry about it. You'll find something. In your field . . ."

"I'm not worried."

"It's better to keep busy," Leonard said. "Keeps you from going nuts."

A tablespoon at rest in a pool of grease on a cracked plate. Joe had finished his lunch. He lay back, closed his eyes, laced his hands on his stomach and let them fall into the peaceful rhythm of his afterdinner breathing. His right cheek bunched, curling that half of his mouth ambiguously. The expression was something else he had inherited from his mother. "You know those checks you had your lawyer send us? Mom put half of every one of those into an account for me."

"That's what she was supposed to do."

"You wouldn't have known any better if she didn't. Anyway, she wanted me to go to school. I could have, too. I had the grades for it. But I bought a pickup and took off. Worked a rig in the gulf for a while. Got married in Shreveport. Two years later I was broke. And divorced. So I wasted it, okay?"

"If you didn't, I probably would have. I never remarried, you know."

"Neither did Mom."

"She should have," Leonard said.

The kid had a certain limited genius, control of several painful facts. Leonard excused himself to go into the bathroom, sit on the lip of the tub and light a cigarette.

What did you expect? Left this house eighteen years ago with a pasteboard box under your arm. So what did you expect?

He had gone into Joe's room. The very last thing he did in this house. He'd gone into the boy's room, crouched near his bed. His hand on the little boy's back--sweaty flannel. He'd whispered again and again, "What has she done to us?" He knew now as he'd known then that the child had no answer for him, and that, even as he'd loved the child, he'd faked love also. Slobbering old bastard, whispering mean mysteries in the dark, "My boy . . . Ah, my little boy." Then the boy had enough. The child Joe rolled over to show that he was awake, that he'd been awake all along. He asked nothing, said nothing. He did not cry. Joe had just found and held onto his father's forefinger.

"You want to go somewhere and get a drink?"

"I could run down to Donatello's for a six pack," Joe said.

"Nah."

"TV?"

"I hate TV," Leonard said.

"How about cards? You play cribbage?"

"Sure."

Joe produced a deck of cards, some wooden matches for pegs, and a cribbage board cut from white oak to resemble a sea bird. The peg holes were drilled into inlaid strips of something he called whalebone ivory. "I made ten of these. Thought I might be able to sell a few."

"I'd buy one," Leonard told him. "I might buy a couple. They'd make nice presents."

"I'm not sure where the rest of them are now."

Never in any competition had Leonard met so luckless an opponent as Joe. The kid's game was resignation. "Fifteen-two, fifteen-four, and a pair of jacks for six." They ground away at the afternoon. Leonard wondered what things might have been like if they'd met at random, just two men trying to dispose of another day. Joe was a poor companion. But under the circumstances . . . A thief's or a suitor's tremor ran through Leonard, kept running until it wore him out.

Eventually Joe looked him over coolly and said "You're not that much different. You don't look different. Must take pretty good care of yourself."

"I use a good grade of mouthwash," Leonard said.

"So what's your livelihood?"

"My job? I sell real estate. Commercial properties."

"I thought it must be something like that. You don't look like you work for a living."

"I did my share of stoop and grunt," Leonard said. "Now I make money." And he was nothing if not a practical man. "If you're serious about selling this place, there's a few things you ought to do. Varnish this wainscoting, open a window once in a while."

"I can't afford to make any more improvements."

"You can't afford not to make improvements. Everything you put into fixing the place up, you triple that and add it on to the asking price. The more a place costs, the easier it is to sell. It's a quirk of human nature."

"I'm broke," Joe said.

"No, I invest in deals like this all the time. I'll float you a loan, and when . . ."

Joe stood. "You think I'm hitting you for money?" He cleared a stack of dishes from the footlocker and went into the kitchen with them. Leonard heard them rattle in the sink. He followed.

"I'd also take up this linoleum," he advised. "It was ugly to begin with."

"Maybe you're not getting my drift. I don't want any more of your money." Joe rinsed a bowl. "What time is it? You want to listen to some tunes?"

Joe's music prevented further conversation, but that was the best that could be said for it. They sat at either end of the couch so that it was not difficult to avoid looking at each other. An adenoidal folk singer detailed his losses. There followed a number of recordings that sounded to Leonard like religious zealots meeting in an assembly plant. The muscles in his back constricted. Was this polite? Joe stared into a middle distance, did some tentative drumming on his thigh. Leonard played solitaire and smoked. Finally he got up to lift the needle away from a particularly quivering guitar solo. "Stuff's driving me up the wall," he said.

"It's about that time, anyway. It's almost time for you to go, isn't it?"

Leonard's foot had gone to sleep. He limped to a window. "You'd think we'd have more to talk about."

"We don't have that much in common," Joe said.

"Well, maybe more than you . . . I think I came up with a pretty good idea while we were sitting here." Leonard fingered the leaves of a sagging coleus and filled his lungs with the rancid air. "You could use a job, couldn't you?"

"A job."

"Yeah. I've been wanting to open up a new office in Escondido. Things are hot as a pistol down there, but I haven't been able to find anybody I trust enough to run an operation like that. If you got your license--and a shave, you could make out like a bandit. We both could."

"Shit."

"You've had a better offer?"

"What do you want from me, Leonard?"

"Do me a favor, don't call me Leonard."

"What do I call you? Daddy?"

"I wouldn't mind getting to know you, Joe."

"I can see it all now. Get out there and throw the old pill around. Go to the zoo on Sundays. Why don't you just rent one of those African orphans?" He pulled his key chain from a pants pocket. Pennies dribbled out.

Leonard got his trenchcoat and followed him out the front door. On the stoop he caught at Joe's windbreaker. "You know why I left?"

"I know. Come on. Sometimes I have trouble getting the car started."

"You know that kid I used to call ratboy, what was his name?"

"Jay Heeny?"

"One night I came out here to call you in for supper. The two of you were over there in the Sundvolds' yard."

"We don't have time for this."

"Oh, I've got all the time in the world, Joey."

"Well, you can use it . . ."

"He was giving you a hard time," Leonard said, "shoving you around. I felt like going over and twisting his head off. But then you grabbed him by the wrists. Man, that was great. You were really strong. You had him. Kid didn't know whether to shit or go blind."

Joe toed a loose chunk of cement at the corner of the step. "If there's a point to this, why don't you get to it."

"You had him by the wrists. You remember what you said?"

"I barely remember Jay Heeny."

"You said 'Please,' and you let him go."

"And?"

"That's when I knew," Leonard said quietly. "That's when it hit me."

"That I was . . ."

"I knew she'd been with another man. That's when I knew you weren't . . . you weren't mine."

"I don't get it. You must have suspected something before that."

"You were such a beautiful little boy."

They crossed the lawn and got into Joe's car. Joe set his hands on the steering wheel and stared at the dash. "You had to suspect something before that."

"You don't see what you don't want to see," Leonard told him. "It's like cancer. You pretend it isn't there, then it gets to where you can't ignore it any more. By then it's too late, too big to cut out. In a way, it didn't have all that much to do with you."

"I always thought she told you about it."

"She did--when I threw it in her face."

There was a freeway now, just a few blocks north of Donatello's market. Once they were on it, Leonard lost his bearings.

The sky had cleared and it was a long dusk. They stood in a lounge, watching broad puddles shiver in the wind across the runways. The quality of Joe's silence had changed. Though he wasn't sure he had reason to be, Leonard was ashamed of himself. He knew that he was expected to say something else. Through a whining microphone the passengers of United Flight 63 were asked to begin boarding. "Thanks," he said. "Thanks for the ride. I would have been stranded."

"That's all right," Joe told him. "I wasn't doing anything else."

"And thanks for letting me know about your mother. It was . . . She was a good woman."

"Too good," Joe said, certain on this point.

"You can't be too good." Leonard offered his sweating hand. It was accepted. "If I can offer you some help, there's no reason to be shy about taking it. No, I don't mean the job. Anything. You know. Just anything. I'll send you my address and phone number." He searched his wallet. "I should have some cards in here."

"Maybe I could use some help getting rid of the house." Joe attempted a smile.

Lame smile of a beaten man. Seeing it scoured Leonard with regret. Learn something new every day. Every day, every day, every day.

"Look, I just came up with another one of my famous ideas. No, hear me out. This is a good one. I've got a friend with a place in the desert. A cabin. He says I can use it any time. I know another guy who can get me champagne at wholesale. So I was thinking--if you could get free around Christmas, maybe you could bring down some smoked salmon or something. We could have sort of a desert Yuletide. It's just something to think about."

Joe nodded, started to say something, then simply nodded again and turned to walk back down the concourse to the main terminal.

Leonard moved forward into the boarding tunnel with a crowd of cologned south-bound travelers. He took his seat. A stewardess gave him a condescending smile, a pillow. He closed his eyes and tried to nap.

At thirty-five thousand feet the 737 began to level off and Leonard watched the leading edge outside his window slice into a feeble string of lights along the coast, then into an apparently endless blanket of darkness. The waters below him were well charted, the tides timed, the various currents almost predictable. He couldn't see the Pacific but he knew, of course, that it was there.

THE MELODIST

At birth she was red and wrinkled and hideous. But she was an only child, and soon enough she had been transformed into that solemn little girl at Easter service, the one holding the bail of her wicker basket so primly in both hands. In those years you would have thought her a packet of confectioners' sugar done up in ribbon and taffeta, unless perhaps you were to catch a more privileged glimpse of her and understand that you were in the presence of a lily of the field. Imagine the end of a fall day; leaves are kiting down to tawny lawns, in the air there is the scent of fried onions and a sense of sweet inevitability. Knockkneed as a marionette, she runs along the sidewalk for home, five minutes late for supper. She is utterly happy.

* * *

Lyla sighted down her legs through the vee of her saddle shoes, thinking, no . . . no . . . as if by an effort of will she could make the car change course. This didn't work, but she always tried it. Cowed by the possibility of her parents' silent disappointment, it never occurred to her to simply say that she did not want to go. Her imagination, though, was a place of splendid license. Deep in the finny Plymouth she led a secret life.

Rough boys, shouting, pedaled their bicycles through the dappled sunlight along Fremond Avenue. Streamers of toilet paper hung from a maple tree. Why? Voices welled from the radio, celebrating love regained. This was a big car and when her mother was driving it, it crept along like a cat. No turning back. They passed the school grounds, the row of brick houses, the park where she was sometimes taken to feed ducks, and then the car rocked gently to a stop. Lyla felt like she needed to go to the bathroom. They got out and moved along a walk bordered by nasturtiums and marigolds. Ivy wove through a trellis around the door.

"You're hurting my fingers, honey. Not so tight."

Bling blong, the chime sounded inside, then the rustle of Mrs. Smith coming.

"Well, aren't we pretty today." Mrs. Smith was just so pleased, pleased and surprised to find them standing there at exactly the appointed time. Big as a refrigerator, she moved back to let them enter her dim cloakroom. Lipstick on her teeth. "I don't know how you girls stay so fresh in this heat," she said. "It's almost more than I can stand." Her hand came to rest on Lyla's head.

"Will you mind very much if I'm a bit late picking her up today? I told her father I'd deliver some linen downtown."

"Take as long as you like. She's my last lesson this

afternoon."

Lyla's mother knelt before her. "My little perfectionist. Don't be so nervous, you'll do fine." She rose, smiled vacantly, and was gone.

Mrs. Smith gripped the slim strands of muscle that were Lyla's shoulders and steered her into the parlor. "How in the world did she come by that idea? Perfectionist?"

Lyla was made to sit at the table in the parlor. Mrs. Smith stood over her. The wild sweep of her eyebrows reminded Lyla of the Wicked Witch of the West. "Since we'll have some extra time today, I'll treat you to cookies and milk."

"Could I have some water instead? Milk makes me . . ."

"Children need their milk." Mrs. Smith went in to the kitchen, her undergarments whispering.

The parlor smelled like the flowers that were brought there to die. Sepia light leaked in through a curtained bay window. Along one wall hung pictures of brooding men. Alone here for the first time, Lyla realized that nothing changed in this room from week to week. Pillows arranged in exactly the same way on the settee, spoons displayed fanwise on a velveteen background, pussywillows in a tall urn. The gloom here had been undisturbed for much longer than she had been alive.

"No, dear. A young lady does not rest her elbows on the table. Never."

Lyla was presented with two ginger snaps on a saucer and a tall tumbler containing twelve ounces of warm milk. She raised the glass experimentally to her lips. It was like grass made viscous; the taste lingered even after she'd taken a bite of cookie.

"Such a face. Do you make faces like that at home?"

This was not her home. At home Lyla was not required to drink milk unless it was ice cold and mixed, about three parts to one, with chocolate flavoring. And at home she was adored.

Mrs. Smith's mother came down the stairs from her room. A woman made terribly delicate by age, she shuffled across the parlor and went into the kitchen from which she emerged several minutes later bearing a tea tray, the pot in its cozy. She had not looked at them once. Lyla watched her slowly climb the stairs.

"Drink up. We have work to do. This wasn't meant to take the whole hour."

Lyla tried the milk again. Her obedience fought the truer instincts of her throat and she was obliged to swallow the same mouthful three times. Mrs. Smith stared disgustedly at her. Lyla calculated. Returning the glass to the table, she set it just so. There was a sound like the ringing of a small bell and white stuff slid evily over the polished wood. "Oh," she said.

"That was no accident." Mrs. Smith went about cleaning the mess and considering how much the child had wronged her. She made the chore seem as troublesome as she could.

At the beginning of her lesson, Lyla made herself perfectly erect. She was told to sit still straighter. Beside her on the piano bench, Mrs. Smith generated a peculiar, dense kind of heat. "Wrists loose . . . not limp, loose. Relax. Did you hear me? I said: relax." They began with warm-up for the right hand, "hear-our-song, it's-not-long, how-we-love-our-singing." Mrs. Smith's metallic incantation. Warm-up for the left hand, "Foll-ow-through, what-you-do, you-will-soon-be-happee." Again. Again. Again. And scales.

C major, both hands, two octaves. Up, down. Again. Again. Again. F. B-flat. E-flat.

"No, this note. This black key. This note, this note. You're in a major scale. It's supposed to sound just like all the others. Can't you hear it? Listen, listen to what you're doing."

The keys became slick and elusive.

"If you practiced even half as much as you're supposed to, this would be easy."

"I do. I practice every day." At home there was an upright piano much like this one, wooden scrollwork and decorative brads. It was in the attic. Each day after school Lyla spent an hour mostly staring, learning loneliness. She had already watched four seasons slouch by the mullioned window. Sometimes just touching the piano made her feel bad.

"Emily Nay started taking at exactly the same time you did, and she's already playing duets with me. She may be a bit more talented than you are, but the big difference is that she's willing to practice."

"I practice," Lyla insisted.

"Lying is particularly unattractive in a little girl. So far you've wasted my time and your parents' money. But I've never had a student yet who didn't give a recital, and you're not going to be any exception. There will be no more excuses; you're going to play at my next recital. Mrs. Smith brought forth a folder of sheet music. This, she said, was to replace *Tunes for Tiny Hands*, some of which Lyla almost knew and could make almost songlike. Lyla regarded the new piece of music. "March the Step Away." On the jacket there was a badly colored line drawing of a drum major, head thrown back, right boot and baton thrown skyward, and this principal figure was followed by prancing puppy, kitten, and kangaroo, all in a row, all smiling mysterious smiles. Children, Lyla knew, were supposed to be charmed by this kind of fraudulence.

Mrs. Smith opened the folder and Lyla saw that the notes of "March the Step Away" were about as numerous and intelligible as birds on telephone wires.

"I'm starting with this now," said Mrs. Smith, "because I assume it's going to take you at least the next three months to learn it."

The months Mrs. Smith spoke of stretched before Lyla and on into the blue distance. To further illustrate the cruelty of time, Mrs. Smith wound her metronome and set it to tick away at lento grave. "Slow, but precise," she said. "We'll begin with the left hand."

Lyla sought to form the opening chord.

"That's bass clef," said Mrs. Smith, as if this would be a useful clue. "No. No. Nooooo." She spread Lyla's fingers across . . . "C . . . E . . . G, there. That is very basic, very basic. You've seen this chord so many times before. Now, with the beat, whole notes . . . one, two, three--one, two, three. Now--the next chord is--don't you recognize it? It's--I know you know it. What's the name of the note at the bottom? At the bottom? You're still in bass clef. That's a . . ." Mrs. Smith clapped her hands and made a noise like fire-crackers. Again she spread Lyla's fingers across the keyboard. "G . . . B . . . D," she said. "From the beginning, then we'll move smoothly through this first change."

For half an hour they worked at the chording of the opening line. The task became possible, then comfortable, then dull. Mrs. Smith said that they would now try the right hand part of the same section; she played six bars of dreadful ditty. Simple to the ear, but hard for the hand. Lyla tried it. She could not make it sound like what Mrs. Smith had played nor anything noticably musical.

"You've got the notes wrong, and you've got the rhythm wrong. One, two, and threeeee . . . What are these? Oh! Two flags on a staff . . . two flags. Those are . . . sixteenth notes, aren't they? One-ta-te-tah, two-ta-te-tah? . . . How many times will you have to be told? You don't seem to retain anything from one lesson to the next."

Lyla began again, failed again. Her attempts multiplied, either lagging behind or surging ahead of the metronome. Mrs. Smith reinforced the beat by jabbing her thumb in the small of Lyla's back. The sensation was not quite as clean as pain and, silently, Lyla wept.

"That's quite enough of that. If you're trying to win my sympathy, this is the wrong way to go about it."

In the moment she was given to compose herself, Lyla felt beads of sweat slide deliciously down her ribcage. That she should be so filled with salty liquids, and that they should have such a range of expression--wonderful. She was a little girl, and she didn't need to know the name of every random satisfaction. "This isn't that hard," she said.

"Of course it isn't. I wouldn't expect you to deal with anything really difficult. Now, let's try it again."

Lyla complied, clumsy as ever, but confident.

"You're rushing the beat," said Mrs. Smith. "Again."

As the repetitions of her effort piled up, Lyla discovered an athletic joy in the resistance of her instrument. She began to hammer it in the rapturous style of the virtuosos she had seen on television.

Without being told to, she included her left hand in her renditions. Now there was an underlying rhythm, and she continued, pushing the tempo to and past allegre. Faster, louder. She played beyond the first six bars, and further, ultimately leaving "March the Step Away" completely behind, where it belonged. Her sound was big. Notes poured from her, each of them perfect, each of them supporting a fragile but ineluctable harmony. And inspiration lifted her to a realm of sublime certainty from which she could only faintly hear Mrs. Smith's voice, demanding, then pleading, "Stop. For God's sake, will you stop this?"

GRAY KITTY

Dear Athalie,

Have finally been installed here in a cottage that may have once been a carriage house but was more probably a garage. Tiny, blue-trimmed thing that sits far back from the street behind a copse of fir trees. Reminds me somehow of one of your mother's Blue Willow plates. Funny how the most innocuous objects still threaten to pull me up short. But then, I've always been easily fogged by reminiscence. She is gone, she is not gone. Something about the way I experience this snaps like a shutter. Before I wax too pathetic, let me reassure you, I'm all right. As you say, I was part of a great romance. Suppose I considered it unromantic to imagine that I might survive her. But I have. Sorrow, as it turns out, comes nowhere near extinguishing me. One discovers one has the very rat's fortitude. In time you find you are really rather happy for the chance to just go on. This is all perfectly natural, and not as grim as I've managed to make it sound. Didn't I start this meaning to reassure you? Be reassured. Please. Your concern wrenches me.

Went to Fort Morris yesterday to buy a very small vial of Nembutal (the heartland's night air is not as narcotic as I'd been led to believe), and on the way back I remembered that you'd asked me if it were pretty here. Foolishly, I turned off the main road to sightsee. Dear old Dad, lost in the rolling hills. Amish country, not quaint but strewn with absurdly complicated farm machinery and identical silos. The fertility of the place was stifling, soy beans, cows, chickens. I mean, my god . . . I might have gone ten or fifteen miles without seeing anything distinctive enough to serve as a landmark. Lost and also in a kind of irrational gloom.

So I turned into a farmyard to ask directions. Met a man with a burlap sack who seemed to think I wanted raw honey. He told me that the farm's previous tenant, a failure, had advertised raw honey and now he, the new man, was always being bothered with requests for it. It was a sore point with him. He wanted to know if we city people thought the honey we bought in supermarkets was cooked. I told him I hadn't given it much thought. The sack obviously contained something living, so I asked him about it. Kitties, he said. This fellow made me feel like an emotional spendthrift. Much of his personal history was smeared on his overalls. Kitties, he said. He was on his way to the pond with them.

Well, the whole business stirred some misbegotten human impulse, and I rescued them. Now they are very much under foot. Their instinct is to be stepped on and to be fed. One calico, one entirely gray. Both female I think. Funny swagger about them. Not graceful yet, but they think they are--tails like little guidons.

A mixed piece of luck in the assignment of my office, the school's dance program was cancelled last year and I got their studio. South half of the third floor of a fin-de-siecle brick building (bricks the color of Bing cherries), skylights running its whole length, beautiful parquet floor. As a place to rehearse or give lessons, it is too cavy, round reverberant acoustics. Mirrors and bars everywhere. Sat at my desk and considered myself from three different angles. None were flattering. Must have been a wonderful room to dance in.

Went to dinner at Dean Woodside's home. Was their only guest. Jumpin' at the Woodsides'. Miserable, miserable evening. If I'm ever invited there again I'll either hire a companion or buy a pistol. Woodside and his wife both appear to be parchment on papier maché. Brittle, resentful academics. Extraordinarily easy to offend them. Woodside talks of his homemade beer and sustains long soliloquies in what I guess to be Italian. Very irritating man. Their children, though, were nice. Adopted, I imagine.

You'll be amused to know that I have a standing offer to join the Dean's Bible study group. Only if they show movies. The night Victor Mature slew a host of feckless extras with the jawbone of an ass, that's still my idea of Biblical study.

Gary should be receiving the school's official tee shirt soon. It says, simply, STATE, in block letters. I find it a somewhat sinister garment, but I understand paraphanalia buyers hereabouts were sick to death of BULLDOGS.

About the phone--I'm not getting one. And please understand, I don't mean this as a criticism, but the plots of novels and movies and accounts of your dreams are not--Would you please just guess what I'm trying to say here?

What else? Nothing, I guess.

Dad

Dear Athalie,

A week after my return, there remains about my house a sense of comparative cool, the low wattage of a single personality. I gained seven pounds at your table. All of it pooled at my belly and I look like a gourd tied to a stick. Is there a more unlikely delicacy than turkey?

Lately I've been eating at Billy Woo's. Green tea and egg rolls. Love all those tympanic sounds from the kitchen. Their funny pots, their funny language.

Do you by any chance happen to remember our walks in Calchet park? The swans?

A Mr. Shirl, second fiddle in the faculty chamber orchestra, keeps asking me, When did you retire from performance? I keep naming the date, and he keeps saying that he saw me only yesterday, concertizing at Darius Hill, Thorne, Rusthaven. Seems he used to haunt the seaboard halls. It embarrasses me that I remember each occasion he mentions. Mr. Shirl is enthusiastic for me. Poor man understands himself as merely competent, remembers me as transcendent. But I was good, wasn't I? Nature's own clear-eyed, big-chested piper?

I won't be coming for Christmas. Your family is a fairly efficient machine (something I note with nothing but admiration, though I can see how I've inflected it badly). It's just that I'm not a very willing traveler anymore, and I don't think you should have to anticipate my sunny presence on the eve of every major holiday. You'll discount this, but I want no hospitality . . . no dutiful hospitality, from my family. Don't be confused by this, Athalie. Don't ever be confused. I adore you.

Dad

Dear Athalie,

This week my gray kitten got kittenish with my pushbroom, upset the handle, tried to outrun it as it fell, and received an awful blow to her little head. I believe the poor thing is brain damaged.

I can't help but compare cat husbandry to my memories of child rearing . . . can you ever forgive me for having been such a muddled parent? But I was unused to the notion of actually liking children. I've always wondered what I'd have done if you weren't such a fabulous child. Most children are only innocent to the extent that they are still ignorant of some of the more subtle vices. What's to like about that? Ever try conversation with a four year-old? Usually quite dull.

> "My son, hear the instruction of thy father,
> and forsake not the law of thy mother:
> For they shall be an ornament of grace
> unto thy head, and chains about thy
> neck."

That from Solomon. I take it he's saying that we have a duty to inflict civilization on our progeny, that a parent's job is to tame the beast he brought into the world. But with cats, see, there's not hope of that. One finds oneself simply serving them, and nothing in nature or scripture requires them to pretend obedience or gratitude. Oh, it is a clean relationship. Thanks to Callie, there are now claw marks in everything I own. Perfectly expressive creatures . . . just as you were, my Sweet.

My fellow fellows at the fellowship are mostly Unitarian and obliged therefore to indulge my skepticism, my ignorance. We are all about equally uneasy in the presence of The Book.

Solomon again, " . . . all is vanity." He makes you love that line.

Did I ever tell you about the Reverend Gilhoover? One of your grandmother's longer lived enthusiasms. I forget Gilhoover's denomination, he's likely not to have had one, but his appearance remains quite vivid. The man wore coal black suits, and, in summer, he could sweat completely through one in about five minutes. Face like a glacier. He was very avid in pursuit of my immortal soul. Succeeded only in terrifying me. Since then, everything to do with religion has smelled dusty to me. But I suppose I'm adventurous now in ways that I've never been before. And courageous?

I've been wondering why, my dear, you were never spoiled by your beauty. I have an extremely pretty student who chose one of those things I adapted from Hindemith's violin duets as a recital piece. She is more obviously political than she knows. In what was probably a small violation of music department protocol, she managed to have me play the other part. She is quite used to having her own way, and, whether you like it or not, that makes it very difficult to refuse her. For pretty girls, the world is a thicket of willing hands. She of the turned up nose and the tin ear. At several points during our brief association, I've had all I could do to resist the pleasure of slapping her.

On to family business. It was a big mistake, sending my address to your aunt. The woman has never recognized that we have nothing to say to each other. She'll write to me now, and be hurt when I don't write back. As to your husband, what would you have me tell him? That I'd always secretly wanted my daughter to marry a salesman? That selling automobile lubricants is a noble vocation? Ed is devoted to you, and he is, as near as I can tell, a decent man. But if he's going to be sensitive about his station in life, I suggest he change it.

Dad

Dear Gary,

Here I am with my two kitties. I am the tallest one. Our eyes are not really red.

Are you too old for this? (Is he too old for this, Athalie?)

Anyway, I miss you, Gary.

Grandad

Dear Mrs. Martung,

This is inevitably awkward. As your neighbor, I should probably just gather my courage and come over and talk to you. I'd like to convince you that I'm not the ogre you imagine, but I expect your opinion of me is pretty solidly fixed. Perhaps, given a little time, I can redeem myself in your eyes.

In the meantime, the animal shelter has asked me to contact you. They want you to quit calling them. Your complaints to them are, of course, justified. But there is nothing they can do about the situation, nothing I can do about it. So, please, no more reports.

I know how this must seem. But believe me, it is quite beyond my poor powers to do that cat any harm. Out of deference to your children I will try very hard to control the profanity and screaming. I am mortally sorry at having frightened them. I must say that the police were more understanding than I would have been in their position. I'm sure they expected . . . no, I'm not at all sure what they expected, but it can't have been good. They can't do anything about this, either, Mrs. Hartung. I'm afraid no one can. About what you saw with the broom--that was just a glancing blow, and those bristles have been well used. They're really quite soft. I should also point out that that sound she makes does not mean that she is in pain. Purely as a technical point, I'd also like you to note that I've never tried to strangle the animal. On that score you have been unfair and incorrect.

You can't imagine how she provokes me. But I suppose you shouldn't have to.

Your neighbor

Dear Athalie,

You accuse me of withdrawing into myself. Well, it's not like I was ever a very communicative man. I know that it has been an unconscionably long time since I've written, but there has been a strange turn of events here. I'm going to attempt an explanation.

Where to begin? Remember cats in a sack? The apparently imperiled? The broom tragedy? As a result of all that I've been living for some time now with a vacant-eyed gray kitten. I felt responsible for its life and for the fact that that life had been so diminished. But am I responsible for gravity?

You can't know what I'm speaking of. Back to history. For a long while after the broom incident, the kitty's needs were few. It slept all the time. Foetal sleep. I played with it, cajoled it. Its lethargy was something sadder than I could endure. Found myself devoting a bit too much time to the project. It remained among the living, but that was about all for a good long while.

By the end of January, she was eating willingly. After this upsurge in appetite, her recovery really took wings. Roughly a month later, she had made astonishing gains in strength and ferocity, and she had claimed not only her own, but Callie's food dish. Callie had no access to any cat food in the house; gray kitty would simply not allow her to eat. Callie moved in with the old couple across the street. I think they blame me for her poor shredded ears. I, who am so obviously clawless.

John the Baptist claimed that a light shone in the darkness, and that the darkness comprehended it not. I can believe that.

Gray kitty has now become perhaps the most sensuous creature alive. She is the cat you imagine in the lap of Nefertiti, her face a blunt diamond shape, her long ears implying a preternatural alertness. She appears not to touch the ground she walks on. Ethereal walker. Stuffed, she would be of museum quality. But she lives. That's the whole problem.

During the last cold snap in February, she left the heat register where she customarily lies, came to my bed, and burrowed under the covers. I closed around her, oyster to her pearl; she'd never required any affection or warmth from me before that, never payed much attention to me, really, for all that I had lavished on her. I touched as much of her as was possible. We liked it. We slept that way all night. Her purring, her . . . An absolutely delicious sleep. I'm not certain that it was perverse, but there is a very good chance that . . .

She has a body like a weasel. She can surround you with it.

Everything was fine until I put her down. When we unfolded that first morning and I put her on the floor, she began to howl. Down a fifth, down a third, then back up to the tonic. If she hadn't been recently spayed (something I'd had done to make her more sociable toward her litter mate), I would have thought she'd gone into heat. I reached down to give her a little pat on her bottom, and she raked my palm with her claw. Four wavy slits along my lifeline. I grabbed her. She drew herself in under my chin and began to purr. Very contentedly. I petted her for ten, twenty minutes. But then, I put her down (a chore--she clings, she unsheaths and clings) and she began to howl again. Her little five note aria, repeated three times, then a glissando of sorts. As near as I can tell, she doesn't stop to breathe.

Now she is either in my embrace (the soul of contentment there), or howling. My neighbors tell me that, with all the windows and doors sealed tight, she can be heard three doors away. We are not the block's most popular couple.

Now, of course, it is spring. I have been driven to the limits of my endurance. Furry incubus. This noise. My hearing, you know, is so sensitive.

Often I think that I must be delivered. I have tried to poison her. Please don't consider me extreme. I offer no excuses. At any rate, I wasn't successful. She sniffed her food dish once, then demanded to be let out. She foraged a meal and came back. At least she is quiet while she's hunting. But she always comes back--to Kritter Kill, to flying ash trays, once to a knife.

I find myself waiting for her. Missing her after a

fashion. She comes back. She survives the cruel world outside, then my terror of her, and always finds her way, eventually, back to the safety of my arms. So you need not imagine that I am alone.

Dad

WIDOW SPAHL

Gaylene looked down upon her children. Their sleep-creased faces were framed in matted, sweaty hair, and a sour smell rose from them. Sarah mouthed silent complaints. Henry Jr.'s fat fingers closed around and repeatedly crushed some innocent dream--grasping, grasping. Their need was relentless. Asleep, they were dear and helpless. And asleep, they were sometimes vile. This was a secret Gaylene kept even from herself. She knew that she would always be good to her children, that she would provide them as much certainty as a child can have. But, at moments like this, she also knew there were crusted channels in her heart. Aware of an exaggerated gentleness, she bundled her babies again in the coverlet and backed away from them.

Her home was eight feet wide, a trailer so small and poorly ventilated that she could smell every meal she'd ever cooked in it. Even old conversations seemed to linger in the air. Gaylene wanted to redecorate before winter. She took down the glossy beach, the lion, and the ox cart she'd cut from an issue of National Geographic. With a butcher knife she tore up the living room's three square yards of carpet. Here her husband had scattered the guts of his Electra Glide for repair; the shag was impregnated with steel filings and solvent. His absence, she thought, was making room for many small improvements.

Her impulse temporarily spent, Gaylene went outside to sit on the milk crate that was her front step. When cold from the metal penetrated her jeans, she began to pace. The ground was boggy, as it would be until it froze. Henry's deal. Two acres on a spring--cheap. No well to drill, willows weeping all around. The trailer was another bargain, its aluminum siding dimpled by a hail storm. A few years earlier, Henry had been very convincing on the subject of a real house. They would drain the property, he'd told her, and build a house with an upstairs and a downstairs both. He was going to cut the timber and split the shakes himself. The limitless future had simmered in Henry's head, but he'd never had any talent for the present. She'd been the wife of a man who chose the path of least resistance.

In the yard a tiny red tennis shoe lay where the puppy had rinished ruining it.

Headlights swung down the lane and switched to low beam. Harlan Brattle's truck approached slowly along the muddy ruts. When it stopped, she heard his shoulder slam its door, the dented door yielding. He got out and spoke her name as if it were a whole statement. He came toward her and she said, "Harlan," also without inflection. Nothing more came to mind. She didn't want to look at him, didn't want to look away. Why hadn't he ever grown to a reasonable height? His eyes, right there at eye level. He looked young enough, sure enough, the same as before. It seemed unfair. "You cut your hair," she said.

"They're makin' me enlist. I go next week."

"So I heard."

"After all them years of sweatin' out the draft," he said. "Got that lottery number, and I thought I had it made. My birthday was the three hundred and sixth one they picked. Now this happens, and I'm goin' anyway."

"They make a lot of people enlist," Gaylene said. "Even people who didn't do anything wrong. You've got no room to bitch."

"I'm not bitchin'. What'd you want? Did you want me to go to Deer Lodge, Gaylene?"

As a matter of fact, the principle of punishment was completely lost on her. "I don't think jail does anybody any good," she said. "You remember Bill Borneman? He worked in Dad's garage for a while. He'd been to prison for writing bad checks. All he got out of it was tattooed. Didn't make him any more honest." She pulled at the skirts of her jacket. "If it was like they said, you should've got off scot free. If you were just defending yourself, I don't see how they can make you do anything."

"That's how my lawyer saw it," Harlan said.

"What if you'd killed somebody important?" she asked him. "Then you'd really be in trouble." At a loss, Gaylene was trying out different attitudes. None of them were working. Her anger was general and she was having no luck finding a place to put it. "You look funny without your ponytail," she said.

"Feels pretty good to get rid of it," he said.

Harlan Brattle--the little packet of gristle. Gaylene squared her shoulders and asked him, "What happened?"

"Just what everybody said at the trial. He turned

crazy and got after me with that pool cue. But I had a cue of my own.''

''I know all that part,'' she said.

''I could tell you I'm sorry, but I can't tell you I'd do it any different if it happened again tomorrow.''

''That's not what I'm after,'' she said. ''I want to know what happened to all those times we had together. Didn't that mean anything to anybody?''

Harlan tore a section of shattered safety glass from the windshield of Henry's GTX. It had an odd integrity in his hand, like a swatch of fabric. ''He was tired of bein' Henry. Didn't you notice he'd started havin' more than his share of accidents?'' Harlan flexed the glass and shards of it fell away. ''You want me to take the car to Polson and get this fixed?''

''It needs a new clutch, too,'' she said. ''I'm selling it as is. Dad's fixing up a Volkswagon for me to use. I never really learned how to drive this thing.''

''A person really don't need four hundred horsepower,'' Harlan said.

Gaylene saw a herd of horses running wild on a plain. They ran right on past her. ''I want you to tell me,'' she said, ''how somebody can be here and then, phht--not be here. I've got the feeling that if it wasn't for gravity, there wouldn't be a damn thing holding us on this earth.''

When Gaylene turned the flame up under her percolator, Harlan asked her if her propane tanks were full. They would be soon, she told him. He saw the birthday cake on the counter. Sarah's birthday already? No, little Henry's--tomorrow. Then why only one candle? Because there'd only been one in the trailer, and it wasn't worth buying a whole pack of them when the kid wouldn't know the difference. Harlan went out to his truck and returned with a plastic airplane, wiped it down with a gas-soaked rag. He'd found it at the dump and had been carrying it around behind his seat. He didn't know why. Gaylene opened her refrigerator door to get milk for her coffee.

"Is that what you're feedin' the kids?" he asked her. "Bologna?"

"Bologna, and weiners, and macaroni. It won't kill 'em."

"No, but it'll make 'em stupid."

"We're sponging off Mom and Dad right now," she said. "They can't afford to have us live fancy." She folded down the table from the wall and set their cups on it. "We haven't had any real meat since Henry hit that buck in the Big Draw. He was quite the provider. Come home with road kill and chokecherries, and then drive all the way to Missoula to hock the radio. But then, I guess I didn't marry him for his good sense."

"I'll try to get you some venison before I leave," Harlan told her. He held his cup in both hands, as if its warmth was something he needed to be particularly grateful for.

"Henry had a short life," Gaylene said, "but more fun than most."

"He worked at it," Harlan said. "That's all he worked at."

"You don't have to put him down, just cause he wasn't like you."

"He was lazy," Harlan said.

"It was just that he didn't know what he wanted," she said. "And if he was so lazy, why'd you let him keep working with you? It's not like you couldn't find another sawyer in Elisis." She remembered waking

Henry at four in the morning to send him off to the woods. He'd moan and curl away from her. She'd shake him as hard as she could and his big frame hardly moved at all. "He hated logging."

"What else would he do?" Harlan asked her. "Think he would've liked it at the mill, pullin' green chain? I mean, what the hell was he supposed to do? Run for congress?"

"I was waiting for him to get his wildness out, Harlan. He would've needed me. He just thought there was more to life than work. He always thought he was missing out on something."

Harlan withdrew from his jacket pocket a stack of bills bound in a thick, dirty rubberband. He put it on the table in front of her. A fifty on top. She could not have named its president.

"Remember those picnics?" she asked him. "Going out to dances at Garcen Gulch? Remember when he had that penny-whistle? We never would've done that stuff if Henry didn't drag us along."

"Just a big kid."

"You act like you're the one who should be mad." Gaylene said. She touched the money on the table. "This is what you were saving for your land."

Harlan looked at her in his impatient way. "Don't know if I'd keep this in the bank, if I was you. I never did. It's better if they don't know you've got it. That way, they can't take it away from you."

"They?"

"The IRS," he said. "And you wouldn't want to let the welfare people find out about it."

"I've never been on welfare yet," she said. "And I never will be."

"Glad to hear it," Harlan said.

"I don't need your money, either. You're not responsible for us."

"You'll need this and more," he told her. "You have to live on somethin'."

"This won't make things any better."

"Can't make 'em any worse," he said.

"For you, I mean. This won't make you feel any better."

"You could go to beauty school," Harlan told her. "You were born to go to beauty school."

"Do you have to be snotty about everything, man? I don't even curl my own hair, okay? And you don't have to be snotty. This money is yours. You're the one person I ever met who knows exactly what he wants. And you've worked for it, you should have it."

What he wanted was a place where aspen choked a creek bed and his nearest neighbor would be three miles away. Paradise Bench, he called it. He'd taken Gaylene and Henry there. "What about the chickadees?" he'd asked them. "Up here, you can hear 'em so good, gets to where you can tell one from the other. I'll keep it just the way it is. For all I care, the gophers can dig to their hearts' content. The creek can go ahead and flood if it wants to." His desire for Paradise Bench was a rare and sterile thing.

"It's nice of you to offer," she told him. "But you had plans for this."

"Just take it."

"I don't want to."

Gaylene took Henry's stash box down from the cupboard above the sink. She rolled two joints, Harlan watching her closely. He was strung together with tensions, like so much clockwork, and mistrusted anything that might wind him down. "It's just ditch weed," Gaylene said. "Too much sober is hard on a guy."

"Look," he told her, "you're gonna take this. We don't have any room left to pick and choose. Take it tonight and you'll save me some trouble. You'd save yourself some trouble, too. You'll be needin' this. You shouldn't have to ask me for it."

Gaylene put her fingers on the big bone in his wrist. "What the minister said, that Reynolds guy--I didn't believe a word of it. Did you?"

"You hardly ever see the guy when he isn't standin' around, eatin' somebody's fried chicken and cake. He must know a little bit."

"Betty told me he gave a real nice service--considering."

"Considering what?" Harlan asked her. "You were there. What do you need Betty's opinion for?"

They had both been there. Gaylene, the tearless widow, and Harlan, the pallbearer. Harlan, steady under the weight of the casket. "I keep waiting to feel something," she said. "I don't think it's ever gonna hit me real hard. That's wrong, isn't it?"

"He'd been givin' you a pretty rough time."

"I was married to the guy," she said. "He was gonna be my life."

"You need to grab whatever comes your way," Harlan told her. "Come on and take this. Please."

"Please--that's a new one, coming from you." Gaylene peeled the joint away from her lip. Wheat straw papers. "I'm sorry about what I said before."

"About how I got off? It was pretty much true. I killed him and--here I am. Could've gone a lot worse for me."

She went around to where he was sitting and pulled his head against her hip. He started to resist and she lightly slapped his cheek. Harlan let himself rest against her. "I don't blame you," she said. "I didn't from the start. Even when I first heard about it, I knew it had to be some kind of an accident."

"You said what you said," he told her. "What comes out of your mouth starts in your brain. That's a simple thing. You've got a right to feel any way you want."

"You keep trying to make things simple," she said. "When they aren't. They never are." The dark aftertaste of the smoke in her mouth; Gaylene was free for the moment from wanting to understand. She understood enough. To be happy, you let yourself be happy. To be kind, you . . . She cupped the base of Harlan Brattle's skull in her hand. The newly barbered hair was like velvet.

"There's a story spreadin'," he said. "There's people down in Elisis who can't believe what happened at the Mint happened over nothin'. I've been hearin' that you and me were . . . They're sayin' Henry'd heard we were goin' behind his back. They say that's why he come after me."

"I've heard that one too," she said.

"Where we found the time and the place to do it is what I'd like to find out." Harlan's breath was labored. He tried to pull away from her again. Gaylene wouldn't let him. "In all the time we've known each other," he said, "I don't think we ever spent five minutes alone together."

"Not until now. Why do you suppose that is? Coincidence?"

"You've gotta go on livin' here after I'm gone," he said.

"Yeah. And then what? Who else is my friend the way you are? I don't care what people say. You never have cared what they say. Why start now? The hell with 'em. Who's gonna be good to us, if we aren't good to each other? What are we, people or pinballs?"

"You stoned?" he asked her.

"Not much," she said. "But I am . . . I'm sick of being by myself. And it's all strangers out there, Harlan. I know you." She moved around behind him, ran her hands over his shirt front. She felt of the sunflower seeds he carried in his pockets.

"What you got goin' for you, Gaylene, you're a good person. Try to stay that way, even if it bores you."

"There's nothing wrong with this."

"I didn't say there was. But, once we got started there'd be no good stoppin' place."

"Tonight," she said. "I just want tonight."

"One of us would want more than that. That's always how it goes."

"I've been by myself for a long time--for a long time before Henry died."

"No, Gaylene. You'll wear me down if you keep after this. It wouldn't be that hard, 'cause . . . You're gonna have to let me be. We're gonna forget this happened. Things are already screwed up enough."

"I won't forget," she said.

"I won't either. But I'll try."

"When you leave here," she said, "I know what you'll say. You're gonna shake your head, and you're gonna say, 'Chicks'."

She saw very little of Elisis through her trees, but Gaylene knew when its citizens were going to bed below her by the exquisite absence of their illuminations from the night sky. She had a cigarette. The smoke seemed strangely cohesive in the cold night air. Many galaxies, some so distant and teeming as to seem gaseous. She found herself trying to apologize to a ghost. No point in that, even if he could hear her. Guilt, she decided, was usually kind of fake anyway. She hadn't wanted all that much, hadn't hurt a soul.

So it was settled--she was a decent human being, small consolation. The swirled constellations were before her. Heaven, maybe.

She visited the GTX. Gaylene had heard the litany of this car many times and remembered most of it. She practiced it as a sales pitch. "It's a blue-printed hemi," she said. "Full race cams, glass packs, Holley carbs, a Hurst shifter . . . Sounds like rolling thunder." He never would admit it, but Henry had really liked it when she'd first come up with the thing about rolling thunder.

One night, in this car, they had passed through Arlee at a hundred and forty miles an hour. The little town had just melted in her windshield. "Slow down, Henry. Please, please slow down." The GTX. Her old enemy. It had gotten to the point that her stomach soured every time he turned the rumbling sonofabitch on. But Henry was the kind of man who is quickly forgotten, and this car would bear his imprint longer than most of the people he'd known. That was not her fault. It was sad, though--poor guy--dead and soon to be so alone in death.

One of her babies cried. A single trill, only slightly distressed. Gaylene went into them. She sometimes worried that she could not allow her children any little suffering, that she might be smothering in them the harder instincts they would need. But they were hers for now. And she was theirs. Gaylene picked up her girl. Twenty-five pound Sarah. Not as clean as those stars, not as hot. But so much closer.

BEASTS OF THE FOREST, BEASTS OF THE FIELD

The beginning of winter was Mitchell Lefthand's favorite time. Range grasses gone pale and brittle, slate gray sage--under a low sky the foothills waited for the year's first heavy snowfall, and he knew again that oddly pleasant sense of enclosure. "We'll have good trackin'," he said. His riders, hunched in the seat beside him, were not in a mood for optimism. "I told you guys this heater might go out," Mitchell reminded them. "You should've wore your long johns."

"I'm wearin' all the underwear I own," said Harlan Brattle. "Your wing window's leakin' on me."

"I can't sit on this spring no more," said Vernon Birfato. "It's really pokin' up now."

The road wound through gullies into Morigeau Gulch. They passed a beaver dam and climbed the last long pull onto Paradise Bench where the timberline started beyond a broad field of sunflower stalks. The cab of the truck smelled of wool and gun oil. Mitchell stopped and Harlan got out to open a wire gate. They turned off the road and followed where tires had matted the grass before, down to a creek bottom to break ice as thin as pastry crust and labor up the other side. Mitchell downshifted on the grade, bouncing his shifter off Vernon's knee. "Gear box is a little broke," he told the boy. "I keep missin' second."

"You got ripped off." Vernon was fourteen and opinionated. "What ain't broke on this thing? For three hundred dollars, you should at least get a radio that works."

Cars from other eras lay in the clearing before them, bigfendered, spent. There was an orchard and a plot where the ground had once been broken for gardening. Near a clump of cedars stood a cabin made of broadaxed timbers and sealed with yellow chinking. All around it were sheds for this and that, empty now and sagging toward a kind of consummation. This chunk of land, Mitchell thought, was anxious to reclaim itself. Sweet water and black dirt--yes. And from here, on a clear day, you could see ten miles of valley floor sloping gently east toward a row of low, buff hills; another twenty miles beyond that were the bladed peaks of the Mission Range, granite that turned blue or pink or gray on any whim of the weather. From here you could see as much as your eyes were able to take in. But there was a particular loneliness about this place.

If there were such things as spirits, Mitchell thought, an unfriendly one lived here with the old woman. "Her chimney's not smokin'. She probably ain't even around."

"Her Rambler's here," Harlan said. "She'll be home."

Mitchell got out of the truck. "She won't know what you're talkin' about. She'll sign anything you give her, but she won't know what it means." He leaned back into the cab to lay on the horn. Out of service. "Haloah. Hello the house--Rosie?"

Rose's door eased open and she looked shyly from it,

recognized her company by stages. "Mitch," she said in her quiet, smeared way. "Harlan. Is that Iris' boy, come with you?"

"Vernon's his name," Mitchell told her. "He's a Birfato. One of Paulette and Herman's kids."

"Who are they?"

"You know who they are. Paulette? You gotta remember Paulette."

"Some things I remember, and some things I don't." She approached as far as a warped washtub at the gate frame; once there had been a fence. "Did you bring me bacon?"

Harlan held up a square of butcher paper.

"What about something to drink? Some of them puzzle books?"

"We got some magazines," Mitchell told her. "*Life*s. You like them, don't you?"

She did. Satisfied, as she had been anyway, she went back into her cabin. From a sleeveless dress her bare arms hung like dimpled brown hams; two thin braids fell nearly to her waist.

As a boy Mitchell had chanced to see Rose Valley fight another squaw in a lot between two bars. The old women rolled in candy wrappers, broken glass, and a wealth of healthy flesh, and when Rosie had tired of that sport--forty years past her prime even then--she pinned the other squaw and said summarily, "Quit now. Come on, I'll buy you a piece of pie." Her airy ways. Sometimes, but rarely, she'd known when enough was enough.

Though they were out of the wind, it seemed colder in her cabin than it had outside. There was a Monarch range, all steel and filigreed enamel, no fire in it; not a stick of wood in sight. Hudson Bay blankets lay in a heap on the floor. Rose wrapped herself in them and rolled an oblong cigarette. She sat on the edge of her bed and smoked just fast enough to stay lit, absorbed, never letting the splayed butt of the thing more than half an inch from her lips. The set of solitude was in her eyes again, inviolable. Vernon sat in Rose's only chair and chafed against the lack of conversation.

"You know George Adams?" Rose finally asked them.

Mitchell and Harlan admitted, as they had many times before, that they remembered him.

"Then--you seen him? He called himself an Adams."

They hadn't. Not for years.

"He owes me money," she said. "We were irrigating for Danny Joseph that one summer. Hundred and sixty acres. Flood irrigating, you know, with shovels. That's hard work. Then it was only me. George run off for two months, and then it was just me, irrigating. I wanted something. I forget what it was, but there was something I wanted to buy. I told Danny, 'Keep it. You keep my money so I don't drink it up.' So George come back around in September. Spent a week with me, and then him and all them wages was gone. It was a lot, too. He got off with that whole summer's money."

George Adams grinned from a Polaroid print pinned to the wall above the head of her bed. The colors of the print were faded to light pastels, the sky behind him a false mist. Gone but not forgotten, and a failure even as a cheat. George Adams. Her memory of him made a ready enough companion. A picture of F.D.R. at Yalta hung also, dwarfed by its gilt oval frame. There were windows at either end of the cabin, just two logs deep, and they cast dusty blue columns of light across the room.

"Let's get outta here," Vernon said. "Let's get huntin'." His elders turned their slow regard on him, and the boy retreated, adding, "I jokes. Can't you tell when I'm jokin'?"

"What's your name?" Rose asked him.

"It's what Mitch told you already, it's Vernon."

"You like candy?"

Vernon recoiled at the suggestion. "Candy? What I like is beer."

"I got some Juicy Fruit," Rose said. From her Prince Albert tin she took a yellow foil packet and handed it to him. Confused, Vernon accepted the packet. It contained a few crimped strands of tobacco. Rose smiled at him. Vernon smiled back, pretended to withdraw a stick of gum, pretended to chew it. This made him very happy with himself.

"Well," Mitchell said to Harlan. "Say what you came here to say."

Harlan Brattle crouched; eye to eye with the old woman, he told her gravely, "We have to cut a new deal. I got in some trouble, wiped out my capital. So I'm gonna have to pay you a little bit at a time. It'll still be interest free, though, I don't believe in payin' interest."

"You're losin' her," Mitchell said. "Keep it simple."

"It can't get any simpler," said Harlan. Then to Rose, a word at a time, "I can't pay you a lump sum like I said I would. Otherwise, it's the same deal as before. The place goes in my name. You can stay here as much as you want, but I want a deed with my name on it. Sign this paper if you like the idea. I can't think of a fairer deal."

"You have that lawyer dream this up?" Mitchell asked him.

"Don't need a lawyer for this. Nobody's losin' nothin', nobody's gettin' screwed."

"You don't write a contract on notebook paper," Mitchell said. "Nobody's gonna take that serious."

Rose made a cup of her hands and whispered something into them. She smiled then as if her hands had whispered back. "I went drinking one night in Polson with them Prettybadger sisters," she said. "Them and Alma Dupuis. We were drinking that Creme de Mint. Boy, that made me sick."

Harlan dragged the heel of his hand down his flat nose. "We can't leave her holed-up here."

"Rosie," Mitchell said, "you better come with us. I'll take you down to Gram's place. She lives in one of them BIA houses now. She could use the company."

"No. Your grandma cheats at cards. Winter would last forever around her." A kerosene lantern sat on her spindly table, its reservoir empty.

"Make her change her mind," Harlan told Mitchell.

Mitchell fitted his watchcap to the top of his head. "She's got no mind left to change. She's went over the edge. You go ahead and do your wheelin' and dealin'. Me and Vernon'll get her some firewood."

Outside, into the moving air. Mitchell sent Vernon off for some wood, then took the dull side of Rose's rusty splitting maul to one of her outbuildings, hammered it apart, broke the boards to stove length and stacked them outside her door.

The old woman had outlived herself; there had been a time not so long ago when she was worth listening to. She had talked about how, when she was a girl, the tribe came up the Clark Fork every fall, harvesting a hundred deer along the way, and how they had wintered around the mineral springs in Elisis or in a place called Big Meadow. Rosie was born and had borne three daughters, all of them lost to her now, in the same teepee at Big Meadow. In those days all the children came in April or May--fitted from the beginning into the right rhythm of the Kasunka. His tribe.

The water people. They weren't warlike. And maybe they'd never really claimed much territory with impunity--before the white man there had been the Blackfeet to contend with--but the Kasunka had wandered the rivers, hunted and fished an enormous ambit, and they had eaten better than anyone in North America. They knew when and where the huckleberries ripened thickest; they netted salmon swimming upstream to spawn; they dug camas root. Mitchell liked to imagine himself wearing deerhide tanned in brains and chewed soft by women. Until well into the '20s, the tribe had led a mobile and, Mitchell believed, a beautifully orchestrated existence. Pretty well ruined now. Sometimes he thought that if he'd only been his grandfather instead of himself, he'd have had an almost perfect life. There was a map of the whole Columbia Basin in his head, an intimation of old Baptiste's restlessness in his heart. Rosie, among others, had planted all this inside him.

She told the stories. She had been of the stories, of that time. But she was also of the misery that had intervened between then and now. Never meaning to, she drew him pictures of a people growing careless. Much of the legend she made of her own endless life smelled of stale saloons, and no one part of her recollection gave her more or less pleasure than any other. Somewhere along the line Rosie had made her peace, made some arrangement with herself that had left her stupid and happy. To Mitchell's mind, another ruinous truce.

He found a sack of lime in the back seat of her Rambler and dumped half of it down her privy. Flies survived there, out of season. Vernon struggled toward him, dragging long, spiny limbs. "Not that," Mitchell said. "That willow won't throw no heat. You'd be lucky to get it to burn."

"That's all I could find."

"Try harder. And don't take so long about it."

"All I wanted to do was go huntin'," Vernon said. "That's the only reason I come up here."

"Why don't you go up the hill and get some real wood?"

"You said: Go down to the creek," Vernon reminded him.

"Now I'm sayin': Go up the hill."

"I wish you'd make up your mind." Vernon turned, leaned hard into the slope, and started to climb. Sullen. A few steps later another mood charged him and he broke into a lope. His bones were obvious through several layers of clothes. Kind of a nervous kid.

Harlan came out of Rose's cabin, looking dissatisfied, and leaned over to blow his nose on the ground. "You better try again," he said. "I hate to think of leavin' her up here. Talk to her."

"Talk to her? You just finished talkin' to her, and where did it get you?"

"She would've signed, but I couldn't get the damn pen to work."

"What's that tell you?" Mitchell asked him.

"Tells me it's too cold for the ink to flow."

"She's nuts."

"She's just been up here alone too long."

"I said she's nuts," Mitchell emphasized.

"She's past takin' care of herself."

"She could do it, if she was interested."

"How you gonna feel if you find her dead the next time you come up here?" Harlan asked him. "Come up here in the spring and find magpies all over her?"

"Everybody dies," Mitchell said. "You worried about her dyin', or worried about her dyin' before you can get your hands on her place?"

"Little of both."

How long you think it'd take 'em to get around any kind of contract you signed with her? You might as well've brought up a crayon, had her put her 'X' on a grocery sack." Mitchell pulled open the root cellar's hinged panel and stepped down into the smell of sex--or damp earth. His eyes adjusted to the dark. "Canned goods," he said. "Peaches--pork and beans. Ten cases each. Sack of mason jars, nothin' in 'em."

"Thing about Rosie," Harlan said, "she don't need much variety. But she's lost a lot of spark here lately. You seen my trees? Used to be, she'd pretty well keep the bears out of 'em, at least when she was around. Now they're all scratched up, limbs broke off."

"Your trees? Not your trees. Not yet."

"My trees. My garden. Damn right, I'll call it mine. Who else wants it the way I do?"

"Just cause you want it, you think it's yours?"

"Yeah," Harlan said. "That's about it."

"The tribe thinks whitey already owns too much of this reservation."

"I don't plan on dealin' with the tribe. This is just

between me and Rosie.''

''Rosie don't have a clue, man.''

Until Mitchell could find someone else willing to take her on, she was going to be his ward. That much was obvious to him now. Without really wanting to, he recalled another one of those half-digested, half-believed stories, the one about an ancient squaw who slung herself on a young man's back to ford a river; and how the old squaw clung to him after they had crossed the river, and on into the night, until the brave leaned her backward over a bed of burning pitch brands.

Rose waited for him in her cabin, her head double wrapped in a yard of Donald Duck scarf. And when Mitchell told her he'd decided she would have to come with them, she said, a little impatiently, ''Well, yeah. I was wondering what was taking you so long.'' She'd forgotten every intention but leaving.

It was as if the heavens had been nothing but snow; concave flakes about the size of pennies, drifting down. By looking up through them, you could sustain the illusion that you were ascending. Mitchell chose not to be fooled. ''Too much of a good thing.''

''We could really use some tire chains,'' Harlan said.

''I had chains. Lavern Dondanville stole 'em.''

Treacherous surface. They reached a bend in the switchback beyond which the road became still steeper, and well before they'd come to the next turning, they were sliding backward. They slid to a stop.

Vernon freed his head from behind Rose Valley. ''She's smotherin' me.''

''She don't have to sit on your lap,'' Mitchell told him. ''You could sit on hers. Some guys'd really go for that.''

"I'm not sittin' on anybody's lap. She's killin' me. And this spring is diggin' me a new asshole. Let me out; I'll ride in back."

"All of you get back there," Mitchell decided. "I want you to sit over them drivin' wheels."

"You're gonna make Rosie ride in back?" Harlan asked him.

"It ain't like she's not padded. You two can keep her from rollin' around. Pull that tarp over you. We gotta get some weight back there, get some traction."

When they had done as he asked, Mitchell backed down to a level stretch of road. He started up again, slow at first to prevent losing purchase, and as he gained speed, he fed the engine more fuel. Valves slapping. He passed the place where they'd been stopped before, slithered and roared another hundred yards up the incline, and felt through his tailbone that the truck had turned unwilling again. "Hang on," he yelled to those riding behind him. They began to roll downhill. Mitchell stayed off the brakes, made the truck describe a tight slalom, and at the next bend in the switchback they had slowed little, so he cut around it and continued down. They rolled on down until they bounced over a kelly hump, made one last grand swerve, and slammed, still backward, up the bank where the road had been cut away. The engine died and a lovely silence ensued.

Harlan Brattle appeared at his window. "Did you bust my thermos?"

"Everybody all right back there?"

"Fine."

"Rosie's okay?"

"Old gal knows when she's havin' a good time." Harlan said.

So it was that Mitchell and Harlan set out to walk up the face of the mountain. Vernon, left behind to make sure that Rosie didn't wander off, was at the point of tears. For a long time they could hear him calling after them, "Fuck you. Fuck you guys."

They took turns parting a trail through the heavy snow. Fifteen hundred feet above the truck, they entered a stand of timber so thick that most of the snow had caught in the branches above them. Snags grabbed at them, and they walked for hundreds of yards at a time on deadfall, never touching the ground. Elk would have sensed the coming weather and started to migrate down through the drainage. Now that the storm was here, they would have bedded in dense cover. Mitchell and Harlan stalked, stopped to listen, stalked. It was impossible to move quietly, but the woods, dark and close and moss-hung, muffled everything, even the sound of their breathing. Mitchell could hear his heart beating--this weird and fearful intimacy with himself was, he understood, partly what he had come to hunt.

Not too long after they'd entered the timber, the buckbrush rattled somewhere ahead of them. Mitchell made himself still. He waited, asked his senses to work a little harder, smelled elk. The rustling again. Mitchell motioned to Harlan that they were going to follow the sound. It occurred to him that the animal he was trailing had a better nose than his, that it had known of him long before he'd known of it, and that it was probably announcing itself in order to lead them away from the rest of the herd. A man might be a fool to follow, but it would certainly be foolish to hold back. At odd intervals, the snapping of twigs. Either a noble creature or an arrogant one. Mitchell wanted very much to see it.

They were led up the drainage, and across it, and into another, never clearing black timber. Hours passed. The effort of climbing and descending and fighting the understory made their hamstrings and calves burn, then ache. Dusk came on. Then, when there were less than fifteen minutes of daylight left, they broke into a clearcut. Snow had mounded over the stumps. Eerie field of smooth hillocks in the failing light. A bull stood at the far edge of it, roughly two hundred yards off, near where the timber resumed again. He was looking back at them. Rack maybe six feet wide. Thick through the brisket--big everywhere, with a calm also massive. Mitchell saw all this, or imagined he did, in the moment it took him to shoulder his rifle. The bull was gone before he could train his sights on it. There, and not there, exactly as substantial as a dream. Mitchell knew he was going to feel uneasy about this affair for a good long time to come.

"We would've played hell gettin' him quartered and hauled outta here," Harlan said. "We weren't gonna get a shot, anyway. Sonofabitch was just teasin' us."

"If I was meant to get him," Mitchell said, "I would have." And the whole trouble was, he believed himself.

They had all been so cold for so long. In the cab of the truck, skating for home, there was among them a harmonic shivering, a reliance. And also considerable hardness. It was a feeling as complicated as love, maybe love itself. None of them had a thing to say.

Mitchell thought about the people he had fallen in with. It looked to him like Vernon was going to be stupid for a lot longer than he was going to be young.

The kid would run out of excuses for himself some day. And there was Rosie, inviting the fates--the fates never quite kind enough to just go ahead and do away with her. And Harlan, wanting only as much of the world as he could get between his teeth. Everyone he knew was built to suffer. He thought of the processes of nature, how they did not seem to lead to anything. That bull, that bull. Ghostlike now, and safe, but with a season to spend belly deep in the snow, pawing for forage. He'd be real enough, soon enough. He'd be hard among the living with the rest of them. Nature made grace and nature ground grace to nothing.

But Mitchell was cold. Just cold, he told himself.

On the last rise before the final descent to the valley floor, they encountered a cow. She loped along before them in the tunnel formed by the headlights. Not enough sense to turn left or right and let them pass. Once, someone had made a poor effort at dehorning her. Left horn gone, right horn curling down to just short of her rheumy eye. In the grand scheme of things as Mitchell understood it just then, she fit perfectly. "Slow elk," he said. "We're gonna put some meat in my freezer."

"Your freezer's not that empty," Harlan said.

"Look at her teats. She's been dry for years."

"Sure, that makes all the difference."

"You afraid somebody'll come along and say nasty things to us?"

"Well . . . yeah."

Oh, not you're worried about gettin' in trouble? What do you think happens if an Indian cop comes up here and catches us huntin' the reservation with a white man?"

"I wish you'd get off this white man kick."

"That's their rule, not mine," Mitchell said. "Rosie, you don't mind a little beefsteak, do you?"

"I liked it, she said, "when I had teeth. Now I have to boil it with cabbage or something, it's not worth it."

"What about you, Vernon?"

"I'll shoot anything," Vernon said.

Mitchell stopped and gave the boy instructions. "She'll quit runnin' pretty soon. She'll wanna turn back and have a look at us. When she does, put a round right behind her ear. Drop her clean, now. She'll be stringy enough as it is; we don't need to run her all over the country."

The boy got out, rolled open the window in the passenger's side door to use it for a rest, and waited. He was breathing hard and plumes of vapor issued from his face. The cow slowed to a walk. As Mitchell had said she would, she stopped and turned to see what had become of her pursuer. "Let her come around a little more," Mitchell said. Too late.

The report was painful in the cab, sudden and very loud; the Hereford dropped to the road without so much as buckling at the knees. She kicked a bit as residual messages made their way slowly through her nerves. Vernon chambered another cartridge.

"That's enough," Mitchell told him. "Little numbnuts sonofabitch. How dead do you want her?"

"See that? I dropped that thing like a bad habit."

"Yeah, you're deadly," Mitchell assured the boy.

The four of them dragged the cow to the side of the road. Mitchell bled her there, field dressed her lying on her side. Already it was impossible to remember why this had seemed like a good idea. But it would be even worse not to go through with it now. When the cow's innards came rolling out, Mitchell sliced free the liver and handed it to Rose. Rose took it close to one of the headlights and inspected it. "It was healthy," she said. "Prettiest liver I ever saw. You did good, Mitch."

Mitchell looked back at the mound of it in her crooked hands, and he knew that, somehow, the old woman would survive them all. She would live on and on, and one day this trip would be another of her stories. After they had gone, she would make them all mean something.